HOW TO SOLVE YOUR GOLF PROBLEMS

HOW TO

SOLVE YOUR
GOLF PROBLEMS

By The Professional Panel of

Jack Burke, Jr.
Byron Nelson
Johnny Revolta
Paul Runyan
Horton Smith

Published by GOLF DIGEST, *South Norwalk, Conn.*
and distributed by
GROSSET & DUNLAP, *New York*

Introduction

by Paul Runyan

A golfing friend and pupil of mine, a Dr. George Tabor, asked me a short time ago why I did not write an anthology on golf. I replied I would first have to know the definition of "anthology." When I learned the literal translation to be "a complete treatise on a given subject," I was quite flattered that Dr. Tabor felt I was qualified for such an undertaking.

The good doctor indicated that in his work, as a specialist in disorders of the eyes, whenever he was called upon to do a delicate operation, he would refer to his anthology on eyes, looking up that portion dealing with the particular problem at hand. In this way he gave himself a refresher course without going through the time-consuming process of relearning all he had been taught during six years of college.

Now how does this compare with our "How To Solve Your Golf Problems" series? Do we contend that the "How To Solve Your Golf Problems" book is an anthology? Well, I shall answer the second question first by saying, "no." We do not contend that "How To Solve Your Golf Problems" is an anthology, but there is a comparison. In this book a golfer can find the cure for almost any specific ailment in his or her game without having to review the entire golf swing. Thus, I feel that our "How To Solve Your Golf Problems" book is a sort of "condensed anthology" for golfers.

I believe, and I think my fellow authors on Golf Digest's Professional Panel would concur, that it would be possible, though not advisable, for the beginning golfer to learn to play by referring to this compilation of errors and corrections. However, this book is primarily for the player who has been through the overall learning process of acquiring a sound grip, address position, and swing plane, and who is looking for a refresher course for a specific fault. Surely any golfer, regardless of the soundness of his swing or the limit of his experience, knows that golf is not an exact science, and that players will from time to time encounter faults that will need specific treatment. This is the primary purpose of our "How To Solve Your Golf Problems."

I have been teaching golf for 35 years and have done much thinking on every phase of the game. Yet I am willing to admit that reading the theories of Horton Smith, Johnny Revolta, Jack Burke, Jr. and Byron Nelson has added immeasurably to my ability to diagnose and correct my pupils' faults.

The beginning golfer has no reason to expect consistency, because there has been no learning period. The established golfer who has a history of inconsistency shows evidence of a learning period that was either too short, incomplete, or did not include sound basic fundamentals.

Thus, my fellow panelists and our editors feel that in order to make the material in "How To Solve Your Golf Problems" more easily understood and useful to golfers of all levels, an early chapter should be devoted to an explanation of the basic fundamentals of golf. I am both flattered and pleased to have been given the assignment.

There are many aspects of golf that could be termed basic. However, in the interest of simplification and clarity, I feel there are only three basic fundamentals of great importance. The Grip, The Stance or Address, and The Swing Plane, and it is these three which we shall discuss.

In the order in which they are accomplished, but not necessarily in the order of their importance, we will first take up the grip, then the stance, and finally the swing plane.

THE GRIP

The proper placement of the hands on the club, besides securing the club against slippage, allows for the greatest degree of mobility in the wrists and, at the same time, provides the best combination of speed of clubhead, and control of face alignment, both so important in acquiring power and directional control.

For right-handed players, the left hand is first placed with the bell-like end of the club's grip snuggling under the fat heel of the hand. The club's grip then runs diagonally across the palm, touching the last joint of the middle finger and thence across the middle joint of the first finger (Picture #1).

The left hand is then turned over the top of the shaft until the inverted "V" formed by the thumb and forefinger points diagonally across the body toward the right shoulder (Picture #2). Strong players, those with exceptional hand action, may point the "V" between the right shoulder and the right cheek.

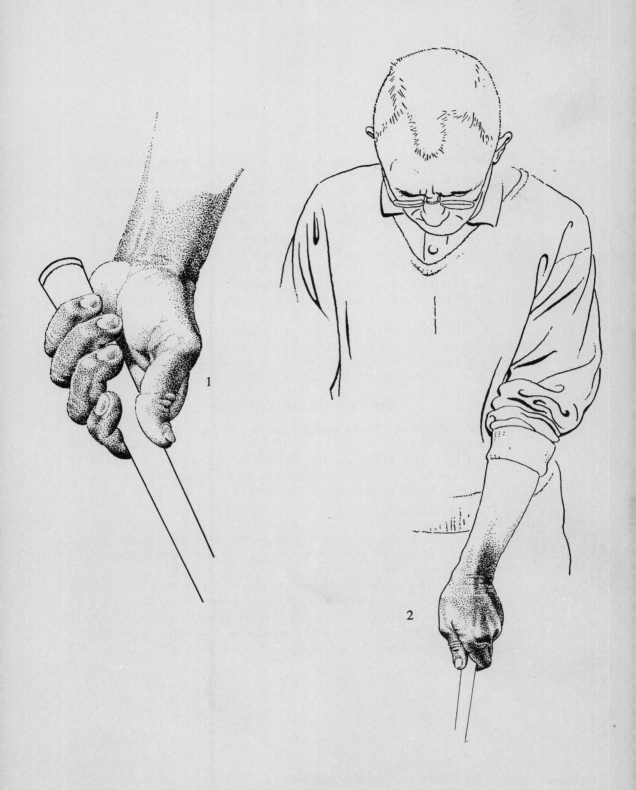

The thumb of the left hand acts as a set screw, pressing against the shaft at an angle of about 30° behind the top of the shaft.

With the left hand in the proper position, we now place the right hand against the back side of the shaft in a vertical position (Picture #3).

Twine the right-hand fingers around the shaft so that the shaft crosses each finger at the middle joint (refer to Picture #3). The little finger of the right hand should overlap the first finger of the left hand, but not hook completely. This is called The Vardon, or overlapping, grip.

For weak-handed women, and the occasional narrow-handed man, a grip in which all eight fingers are on the shaft (Picture #4) may be advisable.

In either grip, the inverted "V's" of both hands should be closed to prevent the club from slipping toward the palm of the hands during the swing. In other words, the thumbs should act as set screws against which the fingers can securely pull the shaft of the club.

THE STANCE OR ADDRESS

In the stance or address position, we are attempting to encourage two fundamentals.

First and most important, the address position should provide a "suspension point" that remains constant during the swing. This "suspension point" is found at the base of the player's neck. It represents the center of the swing arc, the radius of this arc equalling the length of arm and club shaft.

Second, the stance or address position provides the distance the player's head is situated from an imaginary line that extends upward vertically from the ball.

The taller and thinner the player, the closer his head will be to this imaginary vertical line. The shorter and stouter the player, the farther away his head would be. Also the head's position, either behind or in front of the ball, is influenced by the stance or address. This makes it possible for the player to either pinch or lob the shot as the need arises.

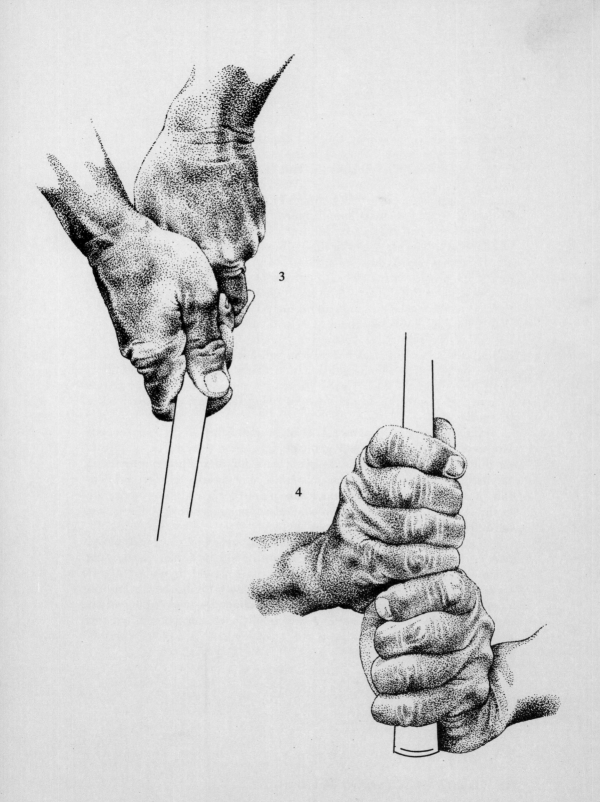

With a driver you play the ball opposite the inside of the left heel with the weight evenly balanced on the insides of the feet. Thus, the head is positioned somewhat behind the ball (Picture #5). This is correct because with the ball teed, the player will strike it about two to three inches after the clubhead reaches the bottom of its arc. This reduces the backspin on the ball to provide maximum distance.

When the ball is lying on the turf as in the case of the 2- 3- and 4-woods, it is advisable to strike the ball nearer the bottom of the swing's arc. If fairway woods were to strike the ball well after reaching the bottom of the arc, as with a driver, a portion of the ball would be below the bottom edge of the clubface. The result would be that full compression of the ball could not be obtained and some power would be lost.

If the ball is played about even with the left heel on the drive, the bottom of the swing's arc comes at a point about two to three inches behind the ball. Thus if we moved the ball back toward the center of the stance by about two inches, this should cause the bottom of the arc to come directly at the ball. This is what we want with the fairway woods, (Picture #6) with the 3- and 4-woods being fractionally farther back in that order.

The long irons are almost as straight of face as the 3- and 4-woods. However, these irons do not generate the same velocity of propulsion on the ball as do the woods. It is not easy for most light hitters to get the ball airborne with long irons as readily as with fairway woods. Therefore, it is inadvisable to play long irons any farther back toward the center of the stance than the fairway woods unless the player desires a very low, hard-flying type of shot.

I advise that the 2-iron be played about two inches inside the left heel with the weight fractionally more on the left foot than on the right. Then each succeeding iron from the 3 to the 9 should be played slightly farther toward the center of the stance until, with the 9-iron for an ordinary type shot, we would find the ball at about the very center of the stance with the weight remaining fractionally more on the left foot than on the right (Picture #7).

If the player desires an unusually high-flying shot for any of the irons, he should move the ball farther forward toward the left foot, keeping the weight evenly balanced between the left and right foot. In this way the ball is swept up off the turf in what is known as a lob shot. Generally, this type of shot requires a reasonably good lie (Picture #8).

One must keep in mind that these high flying lob shots have relatively little reverse spin and therefore do not stop well unless the greens are of sufficient softness for the ball's high flight to bite into the turf.

On the other hand, should a lower-than-average flight of the irons be desired, the ball should be played back toward the center of the stance, with the weight slightly more on the left foot than usual. Then the ball is pinched more into the turf, giving a lower flight with more backspin (Picture #9). One advantage of this type shot is that it works well from a great variety of lies off almost any type of turf from the soft-lush to the hard-packed.

THE SWING PLANE

The third basic fundamental, the swing's plane, is a much misunderstood, highly controversial aspect of the game. This aspect of the golf stroke is influenced most strongly by the degree that the player bends his trunk or torso. The more upright the player stands the more vertical the plane of the swing will generally be. However, the height of the player also has a strong influence on the swing's plane with the shorter player having a flatter plane and the taller one the more upright plane.

The girth of the player is another factor influencing the swing's plane. Of necessity the stout person uses a flatter swing than his thinner fellow player. The short stout golfer will need a flatter plane than the tall stout, and the tall stout will generally have a flatter plane than the tall thin.

The short stout golfer needs a flat swing, first to allow the arms to clear the body during the swing, and second, to produce an arc of sufficient circumference to produce adequate power. This type of golfer needs clubs with a flat lie and shafts of medium to medium-long length to aid in executing this wider arc.

8

9

The short thin player could clear his body with his arms while swinging in a somewhat more upright plane, but in doing so he might dig under the ball. To eliminate this digging, such a player would have to use clubs so short as to cut down the swing's circumference and greatly deplete power. Thus the short thin player should also use fairly long equipment with flat clubhead lies, and he should also swing on a flat plane to produce more power.

The taller stout player should swing on a plane as upright as possible to allow body clearance and adequate power production.

From what has been said about the swing plane one may deduce that I feel a flat swing produces more power than an upright one. This is not true if the upright swing has as wide an arc as the flat one. It is simply a fact that the flatter the plane the wider arc one can use without digging the clubhead into the ground behind the ball. And the flatter plane allows the arms to have greater body clearance, a major necessity for the stouter and shorter player.

Of course the length and lie of the various clubs within a given set, say from the driver to the 9-iron, have a bearing upon the angle of swing plane. The longer driver requires a relatively flat plane (Picture #10). Each succeeding club throughout the matched set to the 9-iron requires a microscopically more upright swing plane because the shafts become shorter and the player stands closer to the ball (Picture #11).

In all cases care must be taken not to become so upright in swing plane as to cause arm friction with the body, clubhead collision with the ground, or power depletion through shortening of the swing's arc.

In summing up, a player will obtain maximum directional control and maximum power if his swing plane is as upright as possible but still not so upright as to produce arm-body friction during the swing.

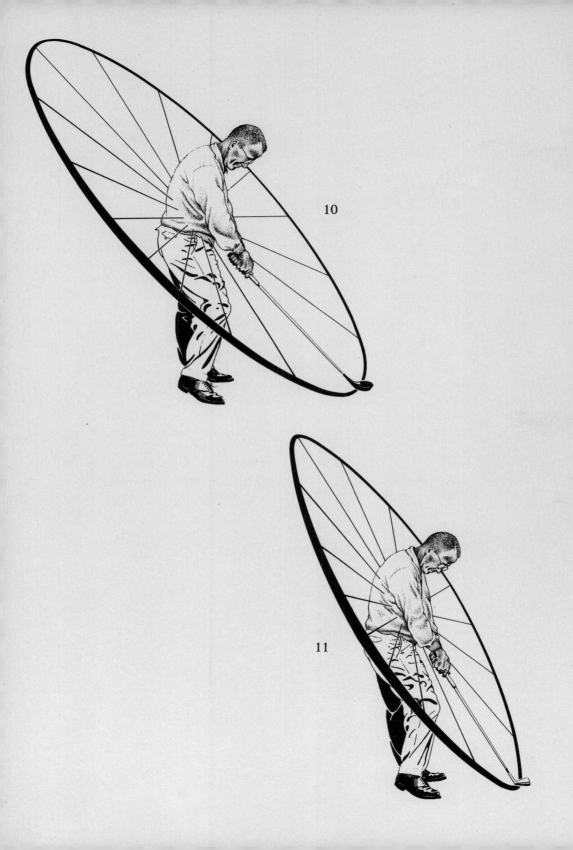

Contents

HOW TO SOLVE YOUR GOLF PROBLEMS

PART ONE

Solving Problems "Off The Tee"

The problems analyzed in this first section are most common "off the tee." There are other areas, naturally, where the same trouble can occur. (One can slice a six-iron with all too little effort). Since the following problems are most evident when driving, they have been grouped together as the first part of this book. They are:

Slicing

Hooking

Pushing

Pulling

Loss of distance

Slicing

by Jack Burke, Jr.

The sliced shot in golf is similar in many ways to the common cold in everyday living. Both are very bothersome.

The slice is double trouble because it not only takes shots off-line, it also cuts length.

Both the slice and the cold are common ailments, infecting everyone sooner or later. Both strike with little warning and often hang on, but both can be cured by sound professional guidance.

However, as with cold sufferers, many slicers soon quit seeking a cure. They resign themselves to living with their disorder, allowing for their shots' inevitable bend to the right.

This is unfortunate because golf scientists have discovered the two causes of all sliced shots:

1. Contacting the ball with a clubface that is "open," or facing to the right of target, rather than directly toward it, and/or . . .

2. Cutting across the ball from outside to inside, thus producing a clockwise spin (counter-clockwise for left-handers).

There are many faults in the golf swing that can produce either or both of these basic causes of the slice. On the following pages I will discuss some of these faults and their respective corrections.

I think one or more of these corrections will help you eliminate those banana balls. But even if you are not slicing now, you should find the discussions to be good "preventive medicine."

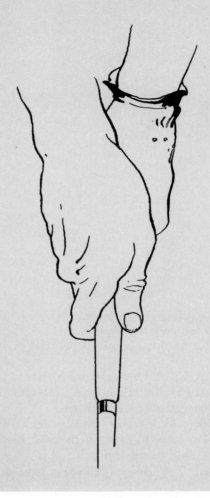

ERROR: "Weak" grip.

In the typical "weak" or "slicer's" grip both hands — sometimes just the left — are turned too far to the left on the shaft. The player sees only one knuckle of his left hand. The "V" formed by the thumb and forefinger of the right hand often points toward the left shoulder.

With a weak left hand grip it is only natural that the player will twist his wrists to the right at the start of the backswing. This opens the clubface so much on the backswing that it becomes difficult to return it to a square or facing-target position at impact. Instead, the clubhead meets the ball with its face still opened to the right and a slice results.

CORRECTION: Grip club with hands turned more to the right.

Grip the club with your left hand so that you can see two knuckles. Grip with your right so that the thumb-forefinger "V" points between your right cheek and right shoulder.

With this grip you will find it easier to start the backswing without independently rolling your wrists to the right and opening the clubface. Instead your hands and arms will go back in unison with the tilting and turning of your shoulders and body. No longer will you be forced to compensate on the downswing by consciously rolling your wrists to the left in order to return the clubface squarely to the ball.

ERROR: Open stance with hips and shoulders turned to left of target.

Many slicers actually compound their problem by aiming to the left of target to allow for the ball's bend to the right. In aiming to the left they pull their front foot back from the target line. This automatically turns their hips and shoulders to the left of target.

From this address position it is difficult for the player to take the club back inside the target line with a normal hip turn. Instead, the tendency is to take the clubhead back to the outside with the hips swaying laterally to the right, rather than turning in that direction.

With the outside takeaway it is only natural that the clubhead assumes an outside-in path on the downswing, cutting across the ball and producing the clockwise slice spin.

CORRECTION: Employ a square stance in which an imaginary line across the toes would parallel a line from the ball to the target.

With both feet parallel to the target line you will find it much easier to take the clubhead back inside. Because this stance will square your shoulders and hips on line with the target, you also will find it easier to turn your hips on the backswing rather than sway them laterally away from the target.

A good way to check to see that your stance is square is to stand opposite a wall in your living room and make certain that both toes are the same distance from the wall. Then assure yourself of an inside takeaway by noting that the clubhead moves away from, rather than closer to, the wall at the start of your backswing.

ERROR: Overturning.

It is a paradox in golf that overturning the hips on the backswing can cause the same problems that result from a sway — or lack of hip turn.

By overturning his hips on the backswing, the player often takes the clubhead too much around his body — too much inside the target line. Then at the top of the backswing, he often loops the clubhead to the outside so that the shaft actually bisects the imaginary target line and points to the right of target.

On the downswing the player then turns his right shoulder almost over the ball instead of bringing it down and under. As a result the clubhead returns to the ball from outside the target line and a slice spin occurs.

Also, because of overturning and transferring so much weight to the right on the backswing, the player finds it difficult to correctly return his weight to his left foot on the downswing.

CORRECTION: Minimize hip turn and weight shift to the right on the backswing.

Too many people feel that a proper turn requires twisting the hips as fully as possible on the backswing. Actually this is not true because such a turn only makes it more difficult to return weight to the left foot on the downswing.

I like to feel that only a slight percent of my weight goes to the right on the backswing. You will be surprised how much your hips can unwind into the ball from a minimum of turn going back.

Also a minimum hip turn will help you refrain from taking the club too far inside on the backswing and then looping at the top. I like to have my club about parallel with the target line at the top of the backswing, rather than to have it looped to the outside so that it points to the right of target.

ERROR: Swaying.

The sway, with its resulting problems, is the No. 1 reason for sliced shots.

In swaying, the player moves his hips to the right much as does a hula dancer. The right leg bends to the right and too much weight shifts to the right foot.

With so much of his weight to the right on the backswing, the player finds it difficult to return his weight to the left on the downswing. Instead he falls back on his right foot before the club meets the ball. This opens the clubface to the right at impact and often forces the club into the ball from the outside. A sliced shot is almost inevitable.

A sway is encouraged by an improper takeaway, wherein the player opens the clubface by twisting his hands and arms to the right early in the swing.

CORRECTION: With right leg firm, turn — rather than sway — hips on backswing.

A proper hip turn will be assured if you do not let your right leg or right hip move any farther laterally to the right on the backswing than they were at the address position.

You will be aided in achieving this goal if you take the club from the ball with your hands, arms, shoulders and body working in a unified "one-piece" movement.

With a proper hip turn you will find it much easier to transfer your weight to your left foot on the downswing. Moving your right knee sharply toward the target at the start of the downswing will further insure against your falling back on your right side.

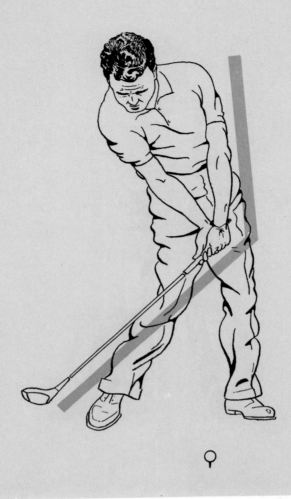

ERROR: Hands too far ahead of clubhead in hitting area.

Sequence photos of professional golfers as they move into the hitting area can mislead the average player.

The pro, with his tremendous hand action and clubhead speed, is able to make the clubhead "catch up" with his hands at impact so that the clubface again looks squarely toward the target.

However, the average player cannot allow his hands to lead the clubhead to such a great extent late in the downswing and still hope to make the clubhead catch up during impact. Instead, his "early hands" and "late clubhead" produce a hit with a still-open clubface that is turned to the right of target.

CORRECTION: Accelerate clubhead on downswing.

Ideally, you should strike the ball with your hands and clubhead in the same relative position as when you addressed the ball.

To assure returning the clubhead to this address position before the hands have moved beyond, I suggest you concentrate on accelerating the clubhead as soon as your hands pass shoulder height on the downswing.

This acceleration will not only help you square the clubface with the target at impact, but will also help you shift your weight to your left foot.

Hooking

by Johnny Revolta

It may be of little compensation to golfers who hook, but they are members of a much more elite group than their counterparts — the slicers.

I don't mean that a hook is anything to brag about. Actually a bad hook can raise scores even faster than a slice because a hooked shot carries less backspin than does a slice and, therefore, is more prone to roll on and on, farther and farther off the fairway.

However, I think it is safe to say that all good golfers — including Ben Hogan and Byron Nelson — have fought a hook at one time or other. I doubt that any living golfer ever hit as many practice shots to correct a hook as did this pair of champions.

Most good golfers are more apt to hook than slice because a hook is often the result of too much hand action. Hand action is desirable in golf, but if overdone a hook may result.

Basically a hooked shot bends to the left (for a right-handed player) because the clubface is turned to the left — or closed — at impact. The hooking tendency becomes even more pronounced if the clubhead passes across the ball from inside the intended line of flight to the outside, thus imparting additional counter-clockwise, or hook, spin to the ball. When this happens the poor victim starts playing nearly every shot from the left-hand rough — if he keeps his shots in bounds.

On the following pages, I will point out five basic causes of hooked shots and supply corrections for each.

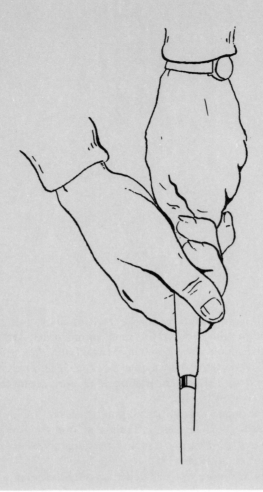

ERROR: "Strong" grip.

A typical "strong" or "hook" grip finds both hands turned too far to the right (to the left for southpaws) on the club at the address position. Such a grip is the most common cause of hooked shots.

Often three or more knuckles of the left hand will be evident to the player. The "V" formed by the thumb and forefinger of his or her right hand will point to the right of the right shoulder.

With this grip the player usually would find that at the top of his backswing the clubface is completely closed, or pointing directly skyward.

From this position at the top of the swing it is almost inevitable that even a normal uncoiling of the body, shoulders and arms will return the clubhead to the ball in a closed position with the clubface turned to the left.

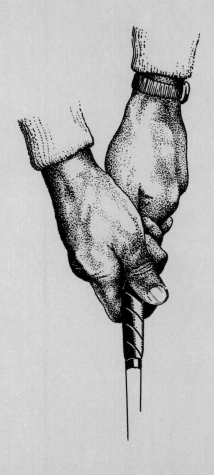

CORRECTION: Grip the club with your hands turned more to the left, holding the shaft more in your fingers.

If your grip is too "strong," you are probably gripping the club too much in the palms of your hands, much like a baseball player grips the bat.

Grip the club with the palm and fingers of your left hand so that you can see only two knuckles at the address position. This should point your left-hand "V" toward your chin. Grip largely with the fingers of the right hand so that the "V" points about to the right cheek.

Now at the top of your backswing you should find your clubface pointing more forward, in the direction that you are facing, not directly skyward as before. A normal uncoiling on the downswing now should return the clubface to the ball in a square-to-target position.

ERROR: "Reaching" for the ball.

Occasionally, hooking stems from standing too far from the ball at the address position.

This "reaching" for the ball may provoke the tendency to take the club too much inside, or around the body, on the backswing. The shoulders tilt little, if any. Instead they turn on too-level a plane, both in going back and in returning to the ball. The player fails to hit down and through the ball. Instead he merely brings the clubhead around his body on the downswing and follow-through in a too-level, baseball-like swing. This forces the right wrist to roll over the left in the hitting area, closing the clubface and causing a hook.

CORRECTION: Stand closer to the ball in a more upright posture.

Standing closer to the ball with less bending from the waist (there should still be a slight bend at the waist and knees) will help you achieve a more upright swing, with less clubhead movement to the inside on the backswing.

Now your left shoulder should tilt slightly on the backswing and your right should come down and under on the downswing. Your hands will automatically go higher on the backswing and follow-through.

All this will encourage your left hand to pull the club into the hitting area and discourage your right hand from rolling over and closing the clubface.

ERROR: Allowing for a hook by aiming to the right of target.

A player who suffers from a hook almost instinctively aims to the right of the target to allow for the shot's bend to the left.

He does this by closing his stance — placing his left foot closer than his right to the target line. In effect, this also aims his hips and shoulders to the right of target.

This player has inadvertently assumed the address position used by many players when they wish to hook intentionally. For a player who already hooks, this closed address position merely compounds the problem.

With a closed stance at address, the player usually takes his club back too much inside the target line. He returns the club to the ball from the inside to the outside. Thus he increases his hooking problems by putting a counter-clockwise, or hook, spin on the ball.

CORRECTION: Address the ball with feet, hips and shoulders parallel with the target line.

Lay a club just outside your ball with the shaft pointing directly at the target — in other words, along the target line. Lay another club parallel to the first and across your toes.

Now, with feet, hips and shoulders facing at right angles to the target, swing through the ball so that the movement of your clubhead in the hitting area parallels the clubs on the ground.

At first you may feel that you are now swinging from outside to inside the target line, or cutting across the ball.

However, keep swinging in this manner and soon your mind and muscles will develop the habit of moving the clubhead along the target line. Very few good players allow the clubhead to move outside the target line at any time during their swings.

Hooking   41

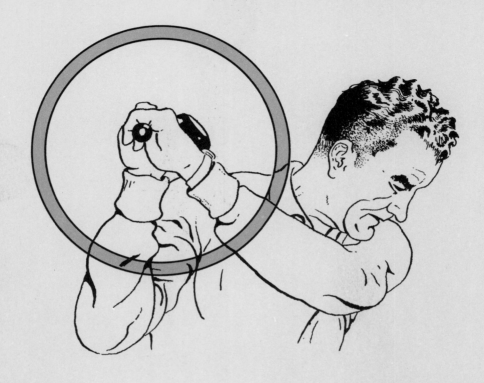

ERROR: Loose left hand at the top of the backswing.

The player who allows the end of his club shaft to slip up into the fingers of his left hand at the top of his backswing is well on his way to a hook.

Failure to maintain a firm grip with the left hand can cause the right hand to dominate early on the downswing.

This right hand domination causes the wrists to uncock too early, when the hands are still well behind the ball.

The right hand overpowers the left, turning the clubface to the left in a hook position when it meets the ball.

It should be noted that the loose left hand can also produce a slice if the player throws the clubhead to outside the target line on the downswing.

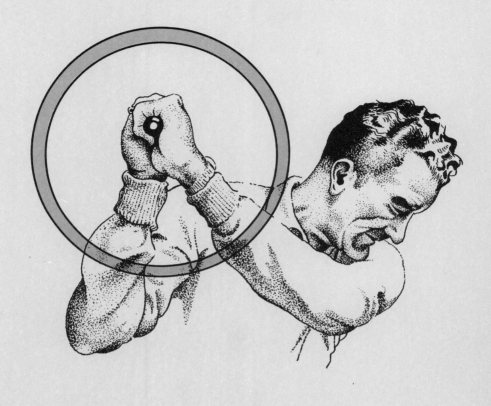

CORRECTION: "Firm up" your grip with the left hand.

Failure to grip firmly with the left hand at the top of the swing can be caused by overswinging — striving for a longer backswing than the player's muscular makeup allows. A shorter backswing will help keep your left hand firmly on the club.

Also, exercises for the left hand will help overcome any right-hand domination. Many have helped themselves by squeezing tennis balls in the left hand. This is very worthwhile, especially in curing a hook, but I feel that a rubber dog bone or something else that fits across the palm in the same manner as a clubshaft will be even more beneficial.

ERROR: Weak or sloppy wrists.

The golfer who is lazy with his wrists, especially as he moves into the hitting area, invites a hooked shot.

Sloppy wrists on the downswing make it difficult for the left side, arm and hand to lead the clubhead into the ball with a delayed unhinging of the wrists.

Instead sloppy wrists encourage the right hand to overpower the left and the hands to lag behind the clubhead at impact. This often closes the clubface into the hook position in the hitting area.

Often sloppy wrists at impact are caused by sloppy wrists on the backswing wherein the hands "drag" the clubhead back from the ball during the takeaway.

CORRECTION: Firm wrists throughout the swing.

Develop the habit of taking the club back from the ball with the wrists firm and the hands, arms and body working as a one-piece unit.

Then on the downswing pull the club down to the ball with a firm left side, arm and wrist. Let your left side and hand lead the club into the ball.

Never consciously try to uncock your wrists into the ball. This usually results in a premature unhinging wherein the right hand takes over and closes the clubface.

Your wrists should uncock automatically as a result of your pulling downward into and past the ball with a straight left arm and a firm left wrist.

Pushing

by Jack Burke, Jr.

The "push" shot is so-named because it actually involves the golfer's pushing or shoveling the ball to the right of target.

Pushing should not be confused with slicing.

The push flies more or less straight, but to the right of target. On this shot the ball adopts little, if any, sidespin.

On the other hand, the slice — because of clockwise sidespin — curves to the right for right-handed players.

The push usually feels good because the clubhead has contacted the ball more or less squarely (as opposed to the glancing blow of a slice).

Actually, the push differs from a good golf shot only in one major respect: The push has the clubhead moving from inside to outside the target line at impact. On a perfect shot the clubhead also moves from the inside, but it then continues momentarily along — rather than across — the imaginary line from ball to target.

There are several major causes of pushed shots. They include improper alignment at the address position; closed clubface at address or on the backswing; failure to turn the hips, and over-emphasis of advice to "keep the head down."

I will discuss these causes in detail and suggest cures for each on the following pages.

ERROR: Aiming to the right of target.

When a golfer addresses the ball so that lines across his shoulders, hips and toes would point to the right of target, he is in an ideal position to push the shot.

When the golfer's body is aimed to the right of target, he will have insufficient freedom to swing his hands and arms through the impact area on a line to the target.

Instead, his hands and arms will tend to swing on paths parallel to the feet, hips and shoulders — paths to the right of target.

The hands and arms will push the clubhead — and in turn the ball — to the right as the clubhead moves from inside to outside, instead of along, the correct target line.

CORRECTION: Address the ball with a slightly open stance.

To cure the push we must make sure that the clubhead contacts the ball while moving along the target line.

To achieve this toward-the-target clubhead movement we must allow the hands and arms sufficient room to move in that direction. The left side must not block their paths.

By addressing the ball with a slightly open stance — with the left foot pulled farther back than the right from the target line — the left side will also be turned clear of the hands' and arms' intended paths.

If this address position is duplicated at impact, the hands and arms will be free to move the clubhead along the target line at impact.

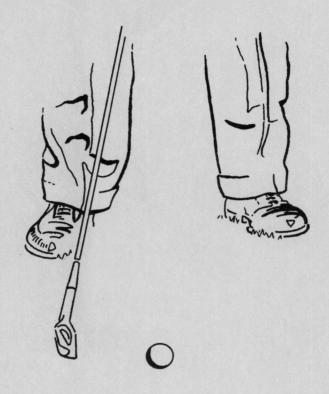

ERROR: Clubface closed at address or early in backswing.

It would appear that the golfer who addresses the ball with a closed clubface (facing left of target), or who closes it on the takeaway, is headed for a severe hook.

However, I'd say that 85 per cent of golfers who see and/or feel their clubface in this hooded position will instinctively compensate. They will naturally open the clubface at the top of the backswing to counteract the impending hook.

This open clubface, along with the golfer's desire to keep the shot from going left, will result in his pushing the ball to the right.

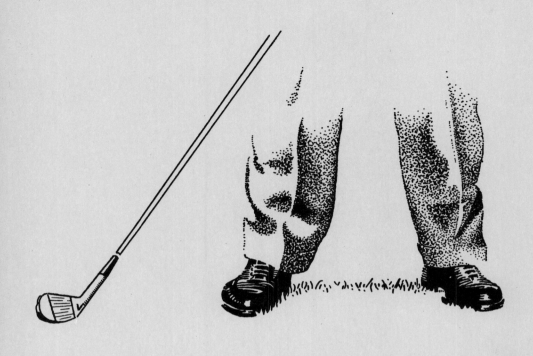

CORRECTION: **Address ball with a square clubface and feel that it opens slightly on the takeaway.**

Normally I would not advocate a conscious opening of the clubface on the takeaway. However, for the player who is in the habit of closing the face going back, this is not bad advice.

Such a player may feel that he is opening the face, but actually he will be taking it back more or less square to the target line.

When the golfer feels that his clubface is already open, he will experience no compulsion to fight a hook. He will not open the face at the top of the swing; nor will he attempt to push the ball to the right.

ERROR: Failure to continue the body turn through impact.

Some "pushers" have the correct address position and takeaway. These golfers usually make their mistake just before and during contact with the ball.

There has been a popular conception that the hips slide into the ball on the downswing. This is true to a certain extent, but if this lateral sliding is overdone a push may result.

If the hips slide, rather than turn, on the downswing, the left hip may block the hands and arms as they move toward the target. In turn, the clubhead will have no chance to move toward the target. It will be pushed to the outside.

CORRECTION: Turn left side to clear a path for the hands and arms.

There is enough lateral motion of the hips and legs in the downswing without consciously sliding the hips.

The golfer should merely move his weight to the left side at the start of his downswing. Then he should let the left hip turn clear of the oncoming hands and arms so that they can move the clubhead along the target line, rather than to the outside.

This turning of the left hip also cushions the force of the swing. The right-handed golfer who finishes with his left ankle bent severely toward the target has probably minimized his hip turn on the downswing.

ERROR: Overemphasis of advice to "keep the head down."

We have already noted that failure to continue the hip turn through impact can force the hands and arms to push the ball to the right.

This failure to turn the left hip out of the way may be caused by keeping the head down for too long a period after the ball has been sent into flight.

Obviously, it is difficult to turn the shoulders and hips when such turning is restricted by a head that refuses to follow suit.

CORRECTION: Allow the head to turn naturally with the follow-through.

I feel it is just as wrong to consciously restrict head-turning on the follow-through as it is to lift the head abruptly before impact.

The head should be allowed to swivel toward the ball's flight as the hands move upward toward the finish of the swing.

By not committing himself beforehand to a rigid "head down" position, the golfer will allow not only his head, but also his shoulders and hips, the freedom they need for proper turning on the down and through stroke.

Pulling

by Johnny Revolta

The pulled shot is one that travels in more or less a straight line, but to the left of target.

Like its counterpart, the push, which flies on a straight line, but to the right of target, the pulled shot usually "feels good" since it is struck with the meat of the clubface in a square, rather than glancing blow.

The pull, though squarely met, goes left because the clubhead is moving from outside to inside, across the target line, during impact. This is directly opposed to the push, which finds the clubhead moving from inside to outside the imaginary line from ball to target.

It is impossible to pull a shot without the clubhead moving in the outside-in pattern.

Thus, to correct a pull the golfer must ascertain what is causing the outside-in swing. He or she must then replace such a movement with a pattern that finds the clubhead moving from inside the target line, to along this line during impact, and then returning to the inside after the ball is away — in short, an inside-in clubhead pattern.

Causes of the pulled shot are usually found in failure to properly coil the body on the backswing: failure to shift weight to the right on the backswing and the left on the downswing, and failure to delay uncocking of the wrists on the downswing.

All of these faults will produce an outside-in clubhead movement and, in turn, pulled shots.

It is not surprising that persons who normally are plagued with sliced shots to the right occasionally discover their shots pulling to the left.

The reason for this is that the outside-in clubhead path is inherent to both the slice and the pull. The only difference between the two is the position of the clubface during impact. In the case of the slice it faces directly at, or to the right of, the target. In the pull it is slightly closed to the left of target.

On the following pages I will discuss in detail specific causes of the pulled shot and supply cures for each cause.

ERROR: Swaying, or moving the body laterally to the right, on the backswing.

As a golfer sways to the right on the backswing, it is only natural that the clubhead may move outside the target line.

Thus, it is likely that the club will return to the ball from the outside. A pull, or a slice, will be the result.

CORRECTION: Coil the body around a fixed "axis" on the backswing.

Imagine that you have a pole running from inside your right foot, up your right leg and through the top of your head.

Then make sure that your head, shoulders and hips swivel around this pole on the backswing, without moving laterally to the right.

The result will be a coiling of shoulder, back and leg muscles which, in turn, will cause the clubhead to move inside the target line.

ERROR: Weight remains on the left side during the backswing.

Failure to shift some weight to the right foot on the backswing often causes a player to shift it to the right on the downswing instead — to fall back on his right foot.

This, in turn, forces the clubhead outside the target line.

CORRECTION: Allow weight to shift to inside the right foot on the backswing.

The player should feel a rhythmical motion that moves his weight momentarily to the right foot.

Then, this weight should return to the left foot immediately at the start of the downswing with a turn of the left hip and a lowering of the left heel.

This proper weight shifting will enable the player to take the club back on the inside and retain it there throughout the downswing.

ERROR: Hitting from the top.

Then we have the golfer who has proper coiling and weight transfer on the backswing, but who jerks the club down to the ball in his anxiety to put the shot into flight.

This premature uncocking of wrists on the downswing destroys the flowing motion of weight to the left side. Instead the weight remains on the right foot and the clubhead enters the hitting area from outside the target line.

CORRECTION: Allow the wrists to uncock naturally into the ball.

The player should feel that everything is moving to the left on downswing in a smooth, unhurried fashion, pulling the still-cocked wrists down and through the ball.

There should be no sensation of forcing the club. The wrists should uncock naturally as result of the uncoiling of the shoulders.

ERROR: "Flying" right elbow.

When the wrists are uncocked too early on the downswing, the right elbow tends to move away from the body. This, along with a poor weight shift, forces the clubhead outside target line.

CORRECTION: Keep right elbow in tight.

If the wrists are allowed to "break" naturally, the clubhead will move from inside the target line and meet the ball squarely at impact. Returning the right elbow to a point close to the body early in the downswing is an aid in this direction. Combine this with a weight shift to the left side and the result will be a straight shot with no loss of power.

Loss of Distance

by Horton Smith

I'm sure that sudden loss of distance has crept into your game at one time or other. I know it's happened to me.

You've been out-driving your weekend golf partners all season. Then one day you suddenly discover that you are short man off the tee. When this occurs it is time to review your swing, preferably under the guidance of a professional.

The golf swing should be a connected and coordinated unit, within which proper timing is paramount. Good timing gives the player all the mechanical advantages which have been built into his equipment. When loss of distance occurs, chances are good that the player's timing is at fault.

However, "timing" is a general term, and proper timing is based on several swing fundamentals. If one or more of these fundamentals are executed improperly, bad timing — and loss of distance — result.

Fundamentals upon which good timing is predicated include: Good posture and balance; proper shifting of weight during the swing so as to achieve maximum control and momentum of the clubhead; and, of course, true alignment of the hands — especially the right — with the clubface both at address and at impact.

Ways to correct any possible short-circuiting of these Basic Requirements for good timing will be discussed and illustrated on following pages. However, first I'd like to suggest a practice technique that has helped me regain distance.

Strangely enough, this involves practicing putts from 5 to 50 feet in length. In such practice, power as such is de-emphasized. The premium is on elements of "precision," such as "touch," timing, square-to-target alignment of hands and clubface, and simply hitting the ball squarely.

Then, when the player progresses from putting to short approach shots to full shots, this emphasis on precision will pay off in added distance.

Thus, putting practice provides a foundation for full iron and wood shots. It's like opening a door — once the key (in this case precise putting) is properly inserted into the lock (your swing), the door (longer drives) opens quite easily.

When practicing putting to build a base for longer drives, concentrate on contacting the ball squarely in the center or "sweet area" of the clubface. Strive for a sharp and crisp sounding "click" as the putter meets the ball. Seek club-ball contact that produces a minimum of jar, shock or vibration.

My friend Frank Walsh used to advise that "as you swing you should train yourself to listen for the click." Anticipating the click serves both as a goal and a check for a precise swing. Try it the next time you play.

In putting, though force is a minimum objective, I am happy to "get distance" without consciously striking the ball hard. The more distance I get on putts with the least effort, the better I like it. This tells me that my stroke is well-timed and in the groove so that the clubface strikes the ball squarely. Then I know that I can expect these same virtues on full shots.

Now let us turn to specific causes for loss of distance and suggestions on how these causes can be eliminated.

ERROR: Shifting weight to the left on the backswing.

Often times, in an attempt to keep the head steady, a golfer will shift his weight to the left on the backswing. He will probably fall back to his right foot on the downswing, sacrificing a great deal of power.

CORRECTION: Shift some weight to the right leg on the backswing.

Make certain that you turn and shift your weight in the same direction as you are moving the club. For right-handed players this would mean that some weight would shift to the right foot in rhythm with the clubhead's move in that general direction.

ERROR: Swaying or lateral movement of the form.

Swaying causes many golf problems, including sliced, topped and "fat" or scuffed shots. However, it is also a major cause of loss of distance.

When, instead of turning his body and shoulders on the backswing, the golfer moves his body laterally to the right, he fails to fully extend or coil the muscles of his left side. When these big muscles of the back and legs are not fully coiled, they fail to generate maximum power to the arms, hands and, finally, the clubhead when uncoiling on the downswing.

Swaying also puts too much burden on the arms which cannot, in themselves, provide maximum clubhead speed.

CORRECTION: Stretch the rubber band.

At one time in our lives most of us have played with model airplanes — the kind that are wound by twirling the propeller which is attached to a rubber band. So it is in the golf swing — except that you are the rubber band.

On the backswing the body should coil or turn, yet still remain in the same area as it occupied at the address position. Generally speaking, the more fully this coiling stretches the left side muscles, the faster the club (like the propeller) will unwind on the downswing.

ERROR: Failure to achieve a straight and taut left arm and a fully cocked right arm at the start of the downswing.

The golfer who starts his downswing with his left arm bent breaks the "circuit" of power which should be flowing from his legs and back muscles to the club. It's like shutting off a flow of water by crimping a garden hose.

Also, failure to keep the right arm bent, or "cocked," at the start of the downswing encourages a premature release or uncocking of the wrists.

CORRECTION: Quick weight shift and a "tight" right elbow.

Return weight to the left foot immediately at the start of the downswing and, at the same time, move the right elbow in close to your side.

These combined movements will automatically cause the left arm to straighten and the right to cock early in the downstroke.

Then, as the clubhead enters the hitting area, the left arm will be ready to conduct power to the club and the right arm can straighten and thrust the hands and clubhead through the ball.

ERROR: Pulling up in the hitting area.

This fault is a result of improper weight shift on the downswing. The golfer has prematurely straightened his right arm and uncocked his wrists well before the clubhead reaches the point of impact. Most all of his power has already been spent.

CORRECTION: Hit down and through the ball.

By leading with the left side and holding wrist "break" until the last possible moment, you save your power for the hitting area. This allows you to achieve the maximum clubhead speed at point of impact and to avoid raising your body in the hitting area.

PART TWO

Solving Problems "On the Fairway"

The problems discussed in this section are usually encountered when the golfer does not have the benefit of teeing up the ball. If the difficulty exists "off the tee" as well, the problem is even greater. In any case, the solution remains the same. The six problems are:

> **Topping**
>
> **Shanking**
>
> **Sclaffing**
>
> **Smothering**
>
> **Grass Cutters**
>
> **Fouling up around the green**

Topping

by Horton Smith

There are three basic elements that determine the success or failure of any golf swing:

— The arc formed by the clubhead.

— The angle or plane of the swing, formed by the arms and club; and determined largely by the ball's position in relation to the stance, the amount of shoulder tilt, and movement of the hands.

— The motion or flow of the swing.

In the case of topped shots — where the ball is usually contacted above center — the basic fault should be charged as an "arc" error. However, the above fundamentals of "angle" and "motion" can spoil the arc, and thus be indirectly guilty.

The ideal swing — one which would seldom produce a topped shot — would find:

— The feet and legs producing a firm foundation for balance and swing power, as well as movement, rhythm, and measurement in returning the club squarely to the ball.

— The left shoulder-arm unit serving as a fixed radius for the clubhead arc from takeaway through impact.

— The right arm hinging at the elbow on the backswing, then straightening (or nearly so) at impact.

In other words, a player would avoid topped shots if he could duplicate at impact a correct address position of his legs, left shoulder-arm unit, and right arm.

Frequently there is no single fault that produces a bad shot; just as no single point, if properly executed, can assure a perfect shot. Often there is a basic fault and several related faults. The big problem or challenge in teaching golf is to detect the basic error.

However, on the following pages I will point out some causes of topped shots in the hope that the reader can play the pro's role and detect the one fundamental error which is causing his or her topped shots.

ERROR: "Scooping."

Probably the most common cause of the topped shot originates in the golfer's mind when he consciously or unconsciously feels that he must scoop beneath the ball to put it into flight. Such thinking is especially common on the pitch shots where the player wants maximum height.

The player then leans or tilts his body to the right on the downswing, apparently trying to put himself "under the ball." This usually restricts the forward motion of the coordinated swing and results in an upward lift or scoop with the arms and hands.

This causes the clubhead to rise abruptly at the ball and frequently catch it above center. An exaggeration of this may lower the right side so much that the clubhead jams into the ground behind the ball. Thus, scooping can also be a cause of "fat" shots.

CORRECTION: Trust the loft of your club.

All clubs, even the driver, have sufficient built-in loft to put a golf ball into flight without any conscious scooping effort on the part of the player.

In fact, a ball is more likely to rise if backspin has been applied to it with a down and through motion of the clubhead at impact. Though it can be overdone, advice to "hit down on the ball" probably will help anyone who has a tendency to scoop shots.

A gimmick, originated by my friend J. Victor East, has helped me convince pupils who don't trust their club loft.

I ask the pupil to hit over some tree branches. He usually tries to scoop the ball and invariably tops the shot.

Then I ask him to hit under the branches. Now he hits the ball correctly with a downward blow, and, to his amazement, the ball flies over the limbs.

ERROR: Improper grip.

Any abnormal grip can destroy the proper clubhead arc and thus produce topped shots. However, the most common grip fault that results in hitting the ball above center is to have the right, or bottom, hand turned too far to the right, or under, the shaft.

This right hand grip has the shaft largely in the palm and directly across it. Such a grip is fine in the baseball swing when a player is trying to contact a ball at, say, chest height.

However in golf, with the ball resting on the ground, this grip merely encourages closing the clubface and lifting the clubhead "over" the ball.

CORRECTION: Proper grip.

In a correct golf grip, the player should grasp the club largely in the fingers of his bottom hand. Thus, when this hand is closed around the shaft, the "V" formed by the thumb and forefinger will point between the player's chin and his right shoulder.

I also advocate that the player see two knuckles of his left, or top, hand when he addresses the ball.

This is the best grip to produce a clubhead path that will connect squarely with a ball that is at ground level.

Even "non-toppers" should develop a proper grip. A bad grip is a direct cause of most swing errors.

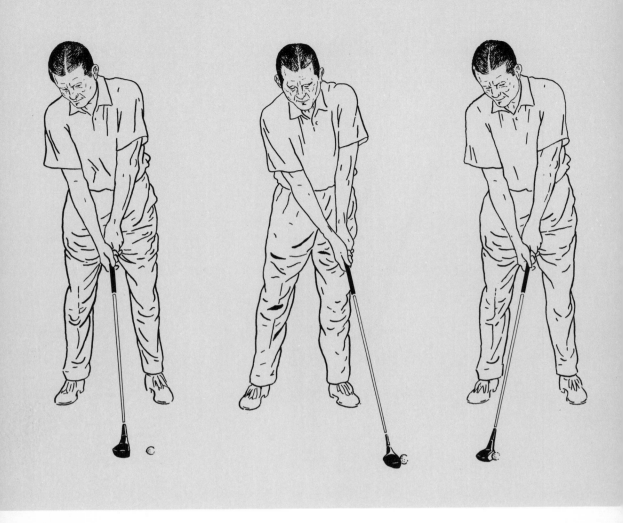

ERROR: Improper positioning of the ball and clubhead at address.

Topped shots can result from any positioning that affects the swing arc. The clubhead, if positioned too far behind the ball (left) will cause the club to meet the ball on the upswing unless swing compensations are made. The same is true when the ball is played too far forward in the stance (center). The clubhead may contact the top of the ball on the downswing if the ball is played too far back in the stance (right).

CORRECTION: Proper positioning of the ball and clubhead at address.

While professionals vary slightly in ball positioning, there is a "safety zone" in which the ball should be played. This safety zone is between the center of the stance and the left heel. When the ball is positioned within this area, and when the clubhead is placed close behind the ball, the swing arc need not be altered; and a square hit should result.

ERROR: Too much crouch at address position.

This problem is more apt to occur with relatively short shots. Thinking he is getting more control by getting closer to the ball, the golfer is actually losing control by forcing the arms away from the body. In this position, there is little hope of controlling the clubhead.

CORRECTION: More upright stance — arms in tight to body.

Allow arms to "measure" the proper distance to the ball. Try to "feel" the arms in close to your body. Then, when starting the backswing, the pivot will help turn the arms naturally to the correct position.

ERROR: Lack of arm and wrist control.

With the arms away from the body and the wrists acting independently, there is little chance that the ball will be hit squarely. There are too many opportunities for the clubhead to stray.

CORRECTION: Square clubhead contact through control of arms and wrists.

The address position should be more or less duplicated at impact. It is comparatively easy to accomplish this if you can think of the wrists as a continuation of the arms, working together in a rhythmic grooved approach to the hitting area.

ERROR: Too much weight on the toes or heels.

A frequent cause of topping is placing too much weight on the toes, either at the address position or during the swing.

This forward weight causes the player to lose some balance during the swing. With his weight forward, he unconsciously tries to regain balance by folding his arms. This, in turn, causes the clubhead to swing "over the ball" and catch it above center.

Too much weight on the heels can also cause the arms to lift the clubhead, though this is not so common a cause of topping as is too much weight on the toes.

CORRECTION: Correct weight distribution at the address position, with the knees slightly bent.

The weight should be equally distributed between the ball and the heel of each foot. If anything, the weight should be slightly "inside" — on the instep side of each foot.

The feet and the legs should be at "relaxed attention" in the address position. As with the runner just before the gun, they should be prepared for action, but not to the point that they are tense.

A slight bending of the knees will help you achieve this feeling. It will enable you to execute a balanced swing wherein your weight does not move too much onto the toes or the heels.

ERROR: Over-emphasizing advice to "keep your head down."

I feel that if taken literally, advice to keep your head down is of questionable value. It can be a major cause of topped shots.

Over-emphasis of "head down" frequently causes such a restriction in the shoulder turn on the down and through swing that the arc is spoiled, and the arms fold upward, pulling the clubhead over the ball.

"Head down" might even cause a player to unconsciously lower his or her head as the club moves into the hitting area. This often promotes a folding of the arms and results in a topped shot.

Naturally the other extreme — looking up — can cause a raising that also lifts the clubhead. However, this is usually caused by indecision and resulting restriction. The mental attitude should be positive and the swing free and trustful.

CORRECTION: Keep the head steady until impact. Then let it turn with the follow-through.

The left shoulder should be rising at impact and the head should be allowed to turn with the club on the through stroke.

The only things that should be truly "down" are the gradually downward descent of the clubhead and the straightening down and through of the right arm.

There should be a sensation of "staying up" with the head, while the arms extend or reach down to the ball.

If a player strives to feel "tall" when he addresses the ball, and then duplicates his address position at impact, he will reach for the ball at impact and avoid the folded arms which produce the topped shot.

Shanking

by Paul Runyan

Shanking — boy is that a nasty word in golf circles! In fact, it's practically taboo among touring professionals to even mention the term.

This habit of hitting the golf ball with the hosel or neck of the club, instead of the clubface, is one of the most demoralizing and most misunderstood of all bad shots.

The shank is a double-edged sword. First, it produces the worst type of shot result. The ball shoots off the club at almost a right angle to the target. The player at the other end of the club can almost certainly expect to lose at least one stroke — and possibly more, if the ball finishes off the fairway.

Second, the shank starts a vicious circle. It creates tension, even in the most skilled, easy-going players. And a tense golf swing, more likely than not, will produce more shanked shots. There is great misunderstanding about the shank. No doubt this lack of knowledge about its causes and cures contributes to this tension.

The shank strikes without warning. It hits good and bad players alike, often in competition when the golfer is under pressure, when his swing might not be in its normal groove. I doubt that any golfer who has suffered through a siege of shanking can watch someone else shank a shot without pondering a similar fate for himself on his next iron shot.

Because the shank produces so much mental anguish, one should not attempt to correct the habit on the course. To attempt correction during a round of play merely increases the chances of harming other phases of one's game. It is best to seek a cure while on the practice tee where one can work under a minimum of pressure.

On the following pages I will discuss the shank's most common causes and cures so that golfers will have a positive plan of action during these practice sessions.

ERROR: Swing has become too flat.

When the clubhead at the top of the backswing points far to the left of the target, the swing is too flat. The swing arc is thus affected and a shanked shot is the result.

CORRECTION: Make swing more upright.

The proper swing finds the clubhead moving along a plane that more or less parallels an imaginary line, running from the ball to the suspension point of the swing at the base of the player's neck. The golfer's shoulders should not only turn, but also tilt, on the backswing.

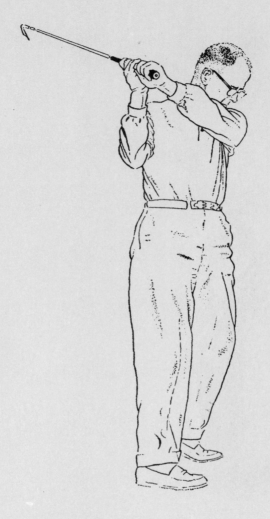

ERROR: Straightening up.

Straightening the body in the pelvic region during the backswing also tends to cause a flattening of the swing. This, in turn, throws the clubhead out of its proper plane during its course through the ball and produces contact with the neck of the club.

CORRECTION: Maintain the suspension point at the same level through-out the swing.

The suspension point at the base of the neck should not move forward or back, or up or down, during the swing.

The player should address the ball by bending slightly from the waist with the knees a bit flexed. Neither the knees nor the back should straighten during the backswing.

Often the tendency to lift or straighten the body during the swing results from over-crouching at address.

ERROR: "Looping."

Looping occurs on the backswing when the player moves his head and shoulders forward and to the left so that they are more over the ball. This also moves his hands and club outside their normal position at the top of the swing so that they too are more over the ball.

This forces the clubhead to return to the ball from the outside, increasing chances for the ball to be impacted at the hosel instead of the clubface.

CORRECTION: Fuller turn or pivot.

This looping tendency will disappear if one takes a slightly fuller turn with his hips and shoulders on the backswing, taking care at the same time not to flatten the swing.

One should feel that his chin remains pointed at the ball, or where the ball was, throughout the downswing and until after the ball is struck.

ERROR: Standing too far from the ball.

    This is actually what a shank is. Once a golfer understands the principle of a shanked shot, there is a tendency to stand farther away from the ball at the address. This increases the problem because the swing becomes even flatter.

CORRECTION: Stand closer to ball and accentuate tilting and turning the shoulders.

By lowering the left shoulder and raising the right shoulder on the backswing, the resulting downswing follows a more upright plane. The clubhead then meets the ball squarely at impact.

Sclaffing

by Paul Runyan

I have heard it said that the Chinese describe golf in somewhat the following manner:

"A game in which the player places a small ball on top of a big ball and, with a club, attempts to hit the small ball into the air without having hit the big ball beforehand."

Confucius may never have won the Fu Manchu Open, but I'm sure he would have appreciated the truth in this definition.

If you hit the big ball (earth) before contacting the golf ball, you are guilty of "sclaffing" or hitting a "fat" shot — a real block to low scoring.

Hitting the ground first is bad on two counts. First, it slows the clubhead an instant before its all-important contact with the ball. Second, it produces poor contact as grass and/or earth come between the clubface and the ball.

There are several causes of, and cures for, fat shots. I will elaborate on some of the most common errors and corrections on the following pages.

In doing so I will refer to the "suspension point" of the swing. This is the center of the golfer's spine at the base of his or her neck.

This is the point of a golfer's body which should be correctly positioned during the swing, lest bad shots — including the sclaff — result. The suspension point should remain constant throughout the swing.

SUSPENSION POINT

ERROR: Crouching at the address position, thus lowering the suspension point.

This is probably the most common cause of fat shots. The player positions himself in an address position that has his suspension point closer to the ball than the total distance formed by the length of his arms and the part of the club below his hands. This crouching, and the lowering of the suspension point that results, causes a bent-arm position at address.

Obviously, if the player maintains this incorrect suspension point position up to and during impact, and if he correctly extends his arms when club meets ball, then his extended arms will cause the clubhead to be lower at impact than it was at address.

The clubhead will cut into the ground behind the ball. Your shot will finish far short of the target, especially if the turf is soggy.

SUSPENSION POINT

CORRECTION: Shorten the swing radius or raise the suspension point.

Because the radius of the swing arc (formed by the arms and club) is longer than the distance from the suspension point to the ball, an obvious correction is to shorten the radius. This is done simply by shortening one's grip on the club — "choking up," as they call it in baseball. The advantage of this correction is that it eliminates the sclaff almost immediately. The disadvantage is that by shortening the radius of the swing, you automatically shorten the swing, and usually lose distance.

The second correction — raising the suspension point — if anything, will widen your swing arc by causing you to address the ball with the arms more extended. More distance may result.

You raise the suspension point by merely addressing the ball with a more upright posture.

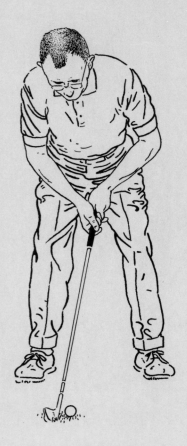

ERROR: Lowering the suspension point during the swing.

Even a golfer with a good posture at the address position may hit fat shots if he ducks his head — thus lowering his suspension point — during his backswing or downswing.

This more subtle cause of sclaffing also causes the suspension point to be closer to the ball at impact than the total length of the swing's radius — the arms and club.

Obviously the player cannot hit the ball squarely with arms extended. He must either hit it fat or fold his arms to compensate for the shortened distance between the suspension point and the ball.

CORRECTION: Maintain a consistent distance from the suspension point to the ball throughout the swing.

The cure in this case is somewhat more difficult to accomplish since it involves avoiding any ducking of the head during the swing.

To keep from ducking the head, I would advise swinging without a club, while your forehead is pressed against a vertical object such as a tree, post or wall.

This will give you an idea of how it feels to swing without lowering your head — in effect, without lowering your suspension point.

Then duplicate this feeling without the post and with a club.

ERROR: Improperly fitted clubs that are too "whippy" for your swing.

Too flexible a clubshaft can produce fat shots even though the player's address position and swing are correct.

Clubs that are too whippy cause a vibratory cycle, or bending in the shaft, which is so great that the clubhead drags along the ground.

CORRECTION: Check shaft flex.

Anyone who has troubles with fat shots should consult his pro about the possibility of using stiffer shafts. This is especially good advice for players who are strong and have forceful swings with a great deal of clubhead speed.

A strong player sacrifices control if he uses too-whippy shafts, just as a weak swinger (women golfers take note) might lose clubhead speed by using too stiff a shaft.

ERROR: During the swing, increasing the angle formed by the arms and clubshaft.

The most subtle reason for fat shots occurs when the player, during the swing, causes the arms and clubshaft to form more of a straight line than they did at address.

In a proper address position the arms should hang almost vertically, at about an 85 degree angle (Angle A'). The clubshaft is supported in a somewhat more horizontal position (Angle C'). Together they form an angle of less than 180 degrees (Angle B').

If, during the swing, the player increases the angle formed by his arms and clubshaft so that they form more of a straight line (angle B), the old principle that a straight line reaches farther than a crooked one of the same length comes into effect. The clubhead extends beyond the ball — or into the ground.

CORRECTION: Maintain the same arm-club angle at impact that you assumed at the address position.

To keep this angle (B′) constant at address and impact the golfer should first address the ball with his arms and clubshaft positioned in about the same manner as in the "correct" drawing above. Arms hang at about an 85° angle.

Then he should maintain the same amount of grip pressure throughout the swing.

If he maintains constant grip pressure during the swing, the golfer will avoid arching his wrists. He will thus be able to hold the proper arm-club angle (B′).

Also one should practice hefting his club vertically in front of him so that he becomes aware of the hand and forearm muscles that increase or decrease angle B′.

Smothering

by Paul Runyan

In evaluating bad shots in the order of their destructive importance to a good golf score, I submit the following:

1. **The shanked shot**
2. **THE SMOTHERED SHOT**
3. **The improperly executed sand shot**
4. **The three-putt green**
5. **The slice**

The shanked shot is most disastrous because it destroys both control and distance and stifles confidence.

Though the explosion shot from sand, when properly understood, is the easiest of all golf shots, it can be a nightmare when poorly executed. However, since we find ourselves in sand rather infrequently, this shot ranks third.

The three-putt green is fourth because it is so demoralizing.

The slice consumes power and destroys control. It might rank second on the list except for the redeeming factor that the sliced shot usually remains air-borne.

The smothered shot, which we shall discuss in detail on this and following pages, does not have this mitigating characteristic of the slice. The smothered shot, when uncontrolled, not only strays violently off-line in the same direction as a badly hooked shot, but it also becomes air-borne only momentarily — sometimes hardly at all. Largely for this reason I rank it second only to the shank on the bad shot list.

It is almost impossible to play well when you are rolling the ball along the ground. I'll take a player anytime who hits the ball only 175 yards but keeps it in flight for 170 yards, instead of a golfer who hits it 200 yards or more, but keeps it in the air for only 150 yards or less.

I make this preference because most God-made and man-made hazards penalize the player who rolls his shots. Aside from tree limbs, there are no hazards in the sky.

However, there is one bright spot with regard to smothered shots. In general they are more easily corrected than are the other villains on my bad shot list. On the following pages I will discuss common causes of smothering and supply a cure for each.

ERROR: Improper grip.

The first and perhaps most prevalent cause of the uncontrolled smother occurs when the player grips the club with his hands turned too far to the right at the address position.

This "strong grip" closes the face of the club on the backswing, resulting in a smothered hook.

CORRECTION: Employ a proper grip.

By turning the hands more to the left, the player can use his wrists properly and still hold the clubface square.

Remember the proper grip has both "V's" pointing to the right shoulder.

ERROR: Playing the ball too far back in the stance.

If the player addresses the ball too far back in his stance, toward the right foot, any normal shift of weight toward the left foot on the downswing will cause the clubhead to contact the turf so far in front of the ball as to smother the shot.

CORRECTION: Play the ball farther forward in the stance.

By simply positioning the ball farther forward — toward the left foot — in the stance, the player will find that the lower portion of his swing arc will occur at the ball instead of too far ahead of it.

Thus, the shot will more readily become air-borne as the player takes full advantage of the club's loft.

ERROR: Moving head and shoulders forward and to the left on the downswing.

In the end the player has moved his head and shoulders toward and to the left of the target during the downswing. This moves the bottom of the swing arc ahead of the ball and closes the clubface so that a low smothered hook results.

I feel that often this incorrect head and shoulder movement is a defensive mechanism. During his swing the player has moved into a position that normally would produce a pushed shot or slice to the right. Unconsciously realizing this, the player compensates to correct the impending push or slice by moving his head and shoulders forward and to the left.

CORRECTION: Proper hand action.

The player must eliminate the push or fade and thus make it unnecessary to compensate by twisting the head and shoulders.

Generally the push or fade can be eliminated by gripping the club correctly and then swinging through the ball with the feeling that the toe of the club is moving past the heel at impact as shown by this exaggerated drawing.

This should cause the clubface to be square at impact. Once the player is confident that he no longer will fade or push, he will no longer find it necessary to move his head and shoulders from over the ball.

ERROR: Entering hitting area with clubface closed.

This is the result of a grip that is too strong. When the wrists are used correctly, the clubface will be closed to face downward and to the left of target.

Thus, the club's loft has become reduced so that the shot nosedives sharply to the left.

CORRECTION: Have clubface square at impact.

If the wrists act properly, and if your grip is correct, the hands at impact will have returned to their address position.

Consequently, the clubface will have returned to its original square-to-target alignment.

Grass Cutters

by Byron Nelson

Many golfers, particularly beginners but also some fairly good players, have trouble getting the ball into the air. They hit "grass cutters," sometimes off the tee but more often on fairway wood shots. These ultra-low shots obviously do not travel as far as they should, and they seek out hazards like a scared bunny heads for the bushes.

Grass cutters often cause golfers to seek escape through the use of more-lofted clubs. True, players who use irons on all fairway shots — and sometimes even for driving — may succeed in raising their shots. However, these golfers are sacrificing potential distance by substituting irons for woods. Also it must be somewhat embarrassing to step out of the crowd and onto the first tee with a 2-iron in hand — when the green is over 500 yards away.

A better solution for someone plagued by grass cutters would be to assay his or her stance, grip and swing for the basic cause of the low shots, preferably under the guidance of a professional instructor.

There are three basic types of club-ball contact that result in shots which fail to attain normal height.

One of these finds the clubface properly aligned with the target at impact, but its loft having become less than normal. An example of this would be the player who has positioned the ball too far back in his stance at address. This player would probably then have his hands so far ahead of the club-head at impact that the club's loft would, in effect, be reduced. Many golfers who wish to hit an intentional low shot use this technique on purpose.

A second type of club-ball contact that will produce a grass cutter has the clubface closed, or turned to face left of the target line, at impact In this position the club's loft again has become reduced and lower-than-normal shots result. An extreme result would be the smothered hook.

The third type finds the club striking the ball entirely above the ball's center. Since it is impossible for such contact to produce much backspin, the ball will nosedive almost immediately, especially if the clubhead was moving upward during impact.

Now, having discussed the types of club-ball contact which will produce grass cutters, I shall point out basic grip and swing errors which produce such contact and suggest ways to eliminate these errors.

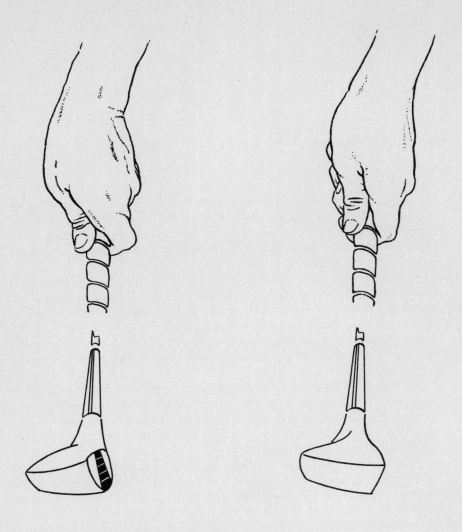

ERROR: Bad Grip.

   The No. 1 cause of shots that roll along the ground is a bad grip position, usually with the left hand. If this hand is turned too far to the right on the club at the address position, chances are good that the clubface will be in a closed position throughout the swing. An extremely closed clubface at impact reduces the club's loft and produces a low shot.

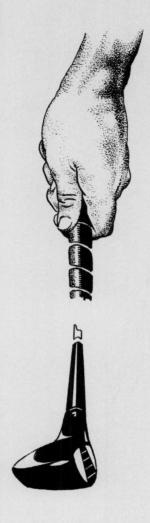

CORRECTION: Weaken the left hand grip.

Make sure that when you grip the club you see no more than one-half of the back of your left hand. If your grip was too "strong" before (left hand turned too far to the right) you may have to adjust by turning the left hand a bit to the left. This grip alteration should eliminate the closed clubface and allow you to benefit completely from the loft which has been built into your clubs.

ERROR: Standing too far from the ball.

The player who stands too far from the ball encourages a flat swing arc. His shoulders will turn on too-level a plane and his hands will not go high enough on the backswing. The clubhead moves too much around the body and not enough up and over the shoulders. With a too-flat swing it is easy to roll the clubface over into a closed position on the downswing. The result is a low shot that hooks badly to the left.

CORRECTION: Let the arms hang comfortably at address.

By standing closer to the ball so that you don't have to reach for it, your swing will automatically assume a more upright plane. Your hands and the club will naturally go over your shoulders on the backswing as your shoulders tilt as well as turn. A long high swing arc will not only increase your clubhead speed and distance, but also it will minimize chances of rolling the clubface closed on the downswing. Higher and straighter shots will result.

ERROR: "Picking up" the club.

We have already noted how a flat swing plane produces low shots. However, it is also possible to hit the ball too low because the club moves too much up and down in the swing. The swing becomes too upright and narrow when the golfer, swinging largely with his arms, lifts his club on the backswing instead of letting it raise almost automatically as a result of tilting and turning the shoulders. Picking the club up will cause it to return to the ball on a sharp downward angle and a low driving shot will result.

CORRECTION: Use a "one-piece" takeaway.

The arms and hands should go back and up as a package in the same motion as the hips and shoulders tilt and turn. As the left shoulder moves down and under the chin on the backswing, the hands, arms and club will raise naturally, without any independent effort. Strive for a wide club-head arc, while taking care to turn — rather than sway — the body. The wide swing arc which results from coordinating the hands, arms, shoulders and body in a one-piece backswing will lessen the clubhead's angle of descent in the hitting area and increase chances for a higher shot trajectory.

ERROR: Consciously trying to lift the ball into flight.

The golfer who feels he must scoop the ball into the air is really defeating his own purpose. In trying to scoop the shot, the player tries to get behind and under the ball. His weight remains on his right foot during the downswing. As a result his wrists uncock too early. Failure to shift weight to the left, along with premature releasing of the wrists, often causes the clubhead to reach its lowest point in the swing well behind the ball. Club-ball contact is not made until the clubhead is moving upward on what should be the start of the follow-through. The clubhead, moving upward, catches the ball in the middle or above the center, thus applying very little backspin. A low, sometimes topped, shot results.

CORRECTION: Trust in your clubs' loft.

Club manufacturers have placed enough loft on clubs so that the golfer does not have to consciously scoop the ball into flight. If the ball is struck with a square clubface when the clubhead is at or near the bottom of its arc, a shot of normal height will automatically result. To assure such club-ball contact make sure your weight returns to your left side at the start of the downswing. Then make the left arm and side guide and pull the clubhead down and through the ball. This weight shift to the left and pulling through the ball will also delay the uncocking of the wrists so as to provide maximum clubhead speed and hand action during impact.

Fouling Up Around the Green

by Horton Smith

In many ways golf has become a game of power. Longer courses, watered fairways, fairway rough and soft greens all give advantages to the slugger, at the expense of the shorter-hitting strategist.

Yet, players who find it difficult, or impossible, to reach greens in regulation figures can still have their "inning."

Skill on chip and pitch shots — say from 40 yards and closer to the green — can put the short-hitter in position to challenge most of his long-driving brethren.

In fact, Harry Vardon, the great British stylist and strokemaker (but a mediocre chipper and putter), once said that "a good approacher and putter is a match for *anyone*."

Certain people are blessed with attributes for "power golf." But I feel strongly that *more* people are endowed with potential ability to succeed in the "precision game" of putting and approaching.

I don't mean that extreme chipping and pitching skill will automatically come to anyone who hits a few practice shots.

I merely suggest that reasonable success is available to every normal person who studies, takes advice (preferably from a professional), practices and utilizes his or her basic resources of sight, feel, muscular adaptation and mental application.

The strength factor is definitely at a minimum in the short game. With that in mind, let us proceed to specific methods that I feel will improve your short shots around the green.

PLANNING THE SHOT

The master technician on shots around the green considers many factors before he ever places the clubhead behind the ball. All of these factors bear on his club selection and shot technique.

He notes how the ball lies in the grass, the amount of green between his ball and the hole, the overall distance from ball to hole, and the contour of the green. He might even consider the texture of grass on the green, any unusual dampness or hardness or softness of the green, and direction and strength of any wind. All this helps him plan and visualize the shot.

The experienced player makes these considerations almost unconsciously as a matter of habit. Any golfer can become as proficient through practice and trial and error.

With so many factors bearing on the success or failure of a chip or pitch shot it is no wonder that many golfers lack a definite plan of action on such shots.

Lack of a positive plan breeds lack of confidence. And lack of confidence has ruined more shots around the green than any other single thing. Often a player blames a scuffed or topped chip shot on "looking up." But most of the time the look-up stems from tension due to lack of confidence — in short, the lack of a plan.

How does one achieve the confidence that goes with a positive shot plan? There are two methods that have proved helpful to me.

LEARNING 'FEEL'

I call the first technique the "part-strength" routine. It is useful not only for shots of 40 yards or less distance to a green, but for all approach shots. It develops a sense of feel within a golfer so that he *knows* just how far a ball will fly and bounce and roll on the green when a specific length of swing is used with a specific approaching iron — wedge, 9-iron, 8-iron, etc.

One must merely practice swings of various lengths with each club until the distances become standardized. For instance, a man might discover that with 9-iron swings of ¼, ½, ¾ and full length the ball flies 25, 50, 75 and 100 yards respectively.

Once this routine becomes grooved, the golfer has a mental yardstick for judging distances during play. Thus, in visualizing and planning the shot he can reach a positive decision of what club to use and how to use it. His mind will be free to concentrate on execution of the stroke and direction of the shot.

A second way to build confidence and a positive plan on approach shots is to select a landing area on the green where you visualize the ball should land in order to bounce and roll to the hole.

This technique is used by almost all leading golfers, just as most top bowlers roll for a spot part-way down the alley, rather than aim for the pins themselves.

Pitching to a spot builds confidence because it allows the golfer to further pre-plan his shot. If the player has developed his "part-strength" routine so that he knows what his clubs will do, hitting to a spot or landing area will make chipping and pitching almost automatic.

On every normal short approach shot to a green, when the green is not unusually sloped or soggy, the golfer should pick a landing spot or area that is about two-club lengths in from the edge of the green.

Choosing a spot this distance into the green minimizes chances that the ball will catch the apron if it should land short of target. Still, this spot is close enough to the player so that he will have to fly the ball only a minimum distance before it lands on the green. Normally, the shorter the distance one must fly the ball, the better will be his control and chances of landing on a selected spot.

The player should use the least-lofted club that will land the ball on the spot and still not allow it to roll far past the cup. It makes sense that if a non-lofted putt is best for shots *on* the green, the least-lofted shot that will not roll far past the hole is best for normal shots *onto* the green.

Of course, unless circumstances do not permit, all shots should be planned to land on the green so that chances of getting a bad bounce will be lessened.

These theories on shot planning — developing the "part-strength" routine and hitting to a spot with the least lofted club — are designed primarily to provide confidence so that the player will visualize the shot and give the ball a positive stroke. However, if a player uses different methods of shot planning I will not quarrel, providing they give him confidence and a visualization of the shot.

STANCE AND GRIP

In putting, there are many different ways to address the ball and grip the club. Yet, there are still certain principles that should be followed. The same is true of the short shot to a green, which in many respects is nothing more than a long putt. Here are some short shot principles:

Narrow Stance: Playing the short shot with the feet close together simplifies the problem of ball placement. A player is more likely to have the ball in position from which it can be struck squarely if his heels are, say, five inches apart than if they were spread 12 inches. A narrow stance also allows the player to take a short swing without shifting much weight or swaying the head and shoulders. This helps promote a square hit.

Square Clubface: The club should face directly along the target line at address. This may sound obvious to many golfers, but I have found that some players "hood," or close, the clubface at address so that the shot will assume a lower trajectory and a minimum of backspin. I'd rather see these players use a less-lofted club and address the ball with a square face.

Hands Ahead of Ball: The hands should be slightly closer to the target than the clubhead at address. This lessens chances of scooping or hitting behind the ball. However, one must not have the hands more than slightly forward at address or he risks striking the ball with too much downward movement and leaving the clubhead in the turf.

Hands Parallel to Clubface: The shorter the shot, the more one's palms should parallel the clubface and be at right angles to the target line. This helps in directing the shot on the intended line. It also minimizes the possibility of rotating — opening and shutting — the clubface during the stroke.

Grip With Controlled Tension: If the hands are too loose on the club, the stroke may become sloppy instead of positive. Scuffed shots may result. Too much grip tension cuts down on the player's feel of the club and often produces a jerky, untimed stroke.

THE STROKE

The short-shot stroke should be a smooth and decisive movement. Whether the results are good or bad, a positive stroke provides a basis of reference from which you can judge future shots. An indecisive, half-hearted stroke teaches little or nothing. Following are some points that will help provide a smooth stroke:

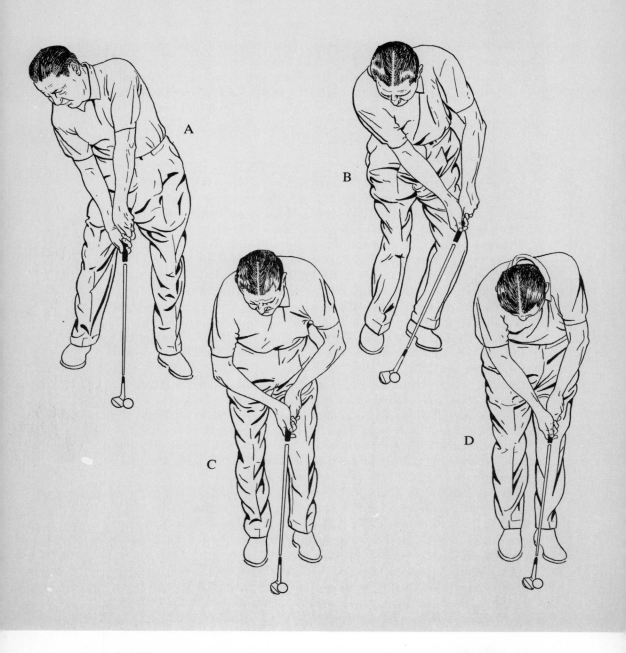

ERROR: Various incorrect positions as seen from in front of golfer.

In figure A, the hands and weight are behind the ball. Figure B shows the hands too far forward. Figure C is incorrect because the arms are "folded"; and in figure D, the golfer's head is too low.

CORRECTION: Assume correct address position.

You'll note the correct address position shows the narrow stance, and the hands slightly in front of the clubhead. It is a fairly upright, yet relaxed position.

ERROR: Too "stiff" at address position.

With the arms extended too far away from the body, the golfer will have little control of his shot. This problem is the result of having the knees too stiff at address.

CORRECTION: More natural address position.

    Stand over the ball more. The knees should be slightly bent and the arms in close to the body. In this more natural position, the golfer can, through practice, learn the "feel" of short shots more quickly.

ERROR: Various incorrect takeaway positions.

In figure A, the club has been taken back too much "inside" or around the body. Figure B is an illustration of an abrupt lifting of the club. In figure C, the hips have swayed to the golfers right; and figure D shows the club being taken back too much "outside," or away from the body.

CORRECTION: Natural takeaway position.

The proper takeaway for short shots has the head steady and the left arm straight. The right arm and the wrists are starting to hinge. The hips rotate slightly but do not sway. Keeping the right elbow close to the body prevents the clubhead from getting too far "outside."

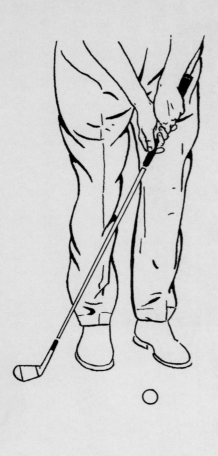

ERROR: Too much wrist action.

By turning the wrists too much on the backswing, the golfer has opened the clubface. On the through stroke, he has rotated the clubface to a closed position. Since there is only one exact point where the club-face is square to the ball, the chance of a straight shot is greatly reduced.

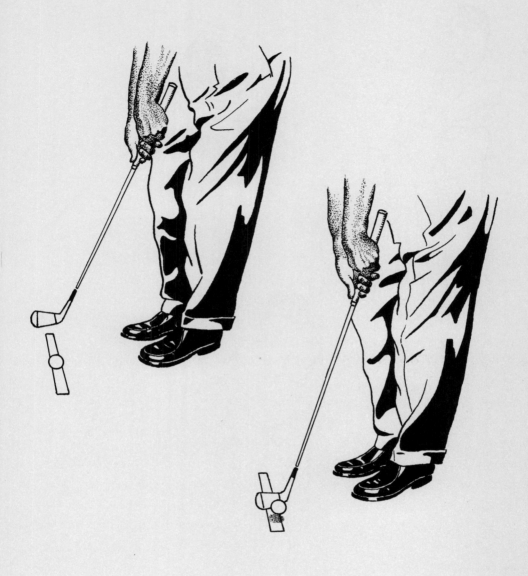

CORRECTION: Keep wrists quite firm.

On short shots, it is possible to take the club along target line with clubface square. Club remains on line with right palm parallel on through stroke. The short shot stroke should be a smooth and decisive movement.

ERROR: Various incorrect follow-through positions.

Figure A shows the hands too far forward, which will send the ball off to the right. In figure B, the head is too low, hindering arm control. This could result in a "fat" or topped shot. Figure C is the all-too-common follow-through pose of a golfer who has tried to scoop the shot by using solely his hands and arms.

CORRECTION: More natural, controlled follow-through.

The natural follow-through on short shots shows the shoulders, legs, hands, and arms moving as a unit with the club. The hips rotate slightly, and the head turns just enough to allow the arms to move freely.

PART THREE

Solving Problems "Here and There"

This section of the book solves an assortment of common golf problems and situations. In most cases, the solutions lie with a basic knowledge of how to analyze, execute, or cope with the particular problem. Presentation, therefore, varies from the "error-correction" format of part one and part two. Here in part three you'll find solutions to problems:

"In the Rough"

"In the Sand"

"On the Green"

"In the Mind"

"On the Scorecard"

Solving Problems
In The Rough

by Paul Runyan

Certain shots in golf puzzle even the expert players. I know that during the early part of my career the most difficult shot for me to execute properly was from heavy, lush grass or rough that was close to a green.

Usually, when I took a firm enough swing to move my clubhead through such thick grass, the ball would fly far beyond the target. When I'd ease up on the shot, my club would stick in the rough and leave the ball short.

One consolation was that most other players, even the finest professionals, also had trouble with this shot.

In this article I will tell how I finally learned to hit this shot. Also I will discuss the best ways to execute other "rough" shots, such as the long shot from heavy grass; the shot from out of a divot mark, and shots wherein the swing is curtailed by obstacles such as boundary fences and trees.

A very important part of "rough" shot playing is not to allow a hazardous spot to discourage you. Once analyzed properly, even the most difficult problem can be solved. If you act hastily, however, taking a chance with the first solution that comes to mind, there's the probability you'll find yourself in deeper trouble. Three or four strokes later you find yourself back on the fairway.

For the remainder of the round you just can't seem to forget that "bad break." This attitude, of course, can throw your entire game off, and you wind up with another one of those "bad days."

So, take your time when in trouble. Try to think of several solutions, even though some may be unique. One will make more sense than the others, and that's the one that will get you "free" with the least penalty.

Now let's get to some specific "rough" shots.

THE SHORT PITCH FROM HEAVY ROUGH

After struggling unsuccessfully with these touchy shots from around greens, I finally noticed one day that Dutch Harrison executed this same shot better than anyone else I had observed. So I set about watching the "Arkansas Traveler" as inconspicuously as I could. Lo and behold the reasons accounting for his superiority became readily evident.

First, during the backswing he lifted his arms and clubhead more abruptly than on conventional shots. This enabled him to contact the ball on his forward stroke while cutting through a minimum of the tall heavy grass.

Also, his swing seemed to go back and forward at a slow-motion pace. When I tried swinging at such a slow pace, the club never seemed to pass through the grass. I either left my shot in the rough or at least short of the target. Yet, when I speeded up my swing, the ball usually went past the hole and often over the green.

So I took another look at the mastery of Dutch Harrison and discovered his secret. To move the clubhead slowly, but positively, through the tall heavy grass, he was gripping the club like iron with both hands and moving his arms slowly, but very firmly, throughout the swing. This ponderous swing moved his clubhead through the heaviest of rough at a speed that would lift the ball, but not fly it past the cup.

Now, if you wish to be really successful out of heavy grass near a green, I suggest you follow the Harrison Method of playing these most difficult shots.

THE LONG SHOT FROM HEAVY ROUGH

Only brute strength can produce much distance from really heavy, lush rough. That's why such strong players as Mike Souchak and George Bayer have the advantage. However, there are some tricks that will help even slightly built men and women players from such lies.

First, the player must carefully note the height of the grass above the top of the ball. Then he or she must select a club with sufficient loft to prevent the grass from entwining the ball as it starts its flight.

Then, as was the case with the short shot from heavy rough, the player must lift his club abruptly during his backswing and then pull it abruptly downward to the ball. Hitting down on the ball with a sharp angle of descent will allow the clubface to contact the ball before club-head speed is slowed by intervening grass.

However, the distance shot from rough differs from the short shot under similar conditions in that maximum clubhead speed is desirable. At the same time the club must be gripped firmly enough to keep the grass from entwining the neck and blade and twisting the club from your grip.

Occasionally a golfer will encounter rough that is so deep and thick that even these precautions will not keep the grass from twisting the clubface into a closed position. Naturally this will produce a shot that travels to the left of its intended direction. Under such conditions I allow for this inevitable closing of the clubface by addressing the ball with the blade turned to the right in a slightly opened position. Also I make it a point to grip even more firmly with my left hand to minimize any twisting of the club.

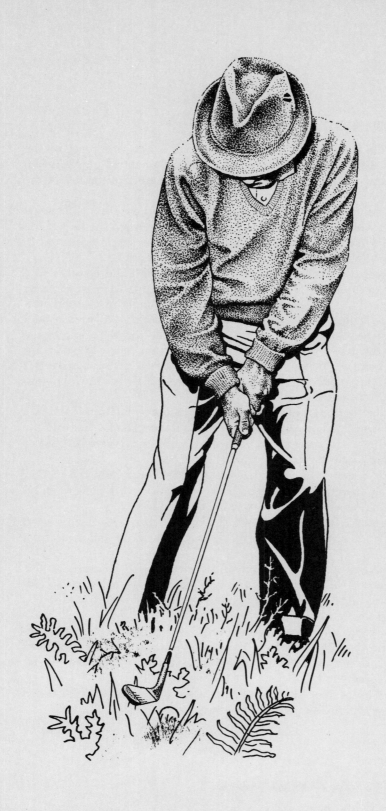

THE FENCE SHOT

First let us consider the shot where the ball is against a fence on the right side of the fairway — a shot wherein the right-handed player is facing the fence. Let's assume that the green is 10 degrees to the left of the fence line.

If the green is 150 yards away, the player should choose a club, say a 5- or 6-iron, which will give him the desired distance when the face of the club is turned inward — to the left — at the 10-degree angle necessary to bring the ball away from the fence at the desired angle.

The player should then make the stroke backward and forward on a line parallel to the fence in order to prevent the clubhead from catching in the fence, all the while retaining the turned-in angle of the clubface.

A rule of thumb would be that the amount of club loft used should lessen the farther the distance to the green and the less the angle of the green from the fence. However, as the angle from fence to green increases, the more the player must close his clubface at address. Since this turning of the face reduces the club's loft, a more-lofted club must be used as the angle from fence to green increases.

By far the more perplexing "fence shot" is that which finds the ball against a fence that runs along the left side of the fairway. Because the right-handed player cannot take a normal swing, he must often be content to merely chip or jab the ball for a short distance.

However, a golfer who is somewhat ambidextrous might try another alternative. By inverting a right-handed 8- or 9-iron, such a player can hit this shot quite successfully with a left-handed swing.

By swinging left-handed and parallel to the fence with this inverted club, the ball will automatically travel sharply to the right and away from the fence.

It is true that no great amount of distance can be obtained on this shot. However, it will cost you on the average only one-half a stroke, instead of a full-shot loss for merely chipping away, or two strokes if you had declared the lie unplayable.

Also, there is the thrilling prospect that if this type of lie is encountered no more than 75 yards from the green, a player who has practiced this inverted shot may actually escape any stroke loss whatsoever by reaching the green.

(These "fence shot" techniques are also applicable to left-handed golfers if they will merely reverse the above procedures.)

THE TREE SHOT

Often a player finds his ball sitting up in a beautiful lie with absolutely no interference between it and the green, but with a tree so close to the golfer that it prevents a normal swing through the ball.

Rather than break a club or injure himself on the follow-through, the inexperienced player might be content to chip the ball away from the tree a short distance, thus sacrificing a stroke. Or he might try a fuller swing, to get more distance. Usually, however, he will flinch to avoid hitting the tree and therefore will completely miss, or at least mis-hit, the shot.

The proper procedure under such a condition is to first select the shortest club (most-lofted) that will provide the desired distance.

Then play the ball off a point just inside the right foot — the foot farthest from the tree — and retain your weight on the left foot throughout the stroke.

Thus, by playing the ball back in the stance and keeping weight forward, the clubhead will automatically lift abruptly on the backswing and descend sharply downward to the ball. The clubhead will enter the turf immediately after the ball has been struck, abruptly arresting the club's forward motion so that contact with the tree probably will be eliminated.

HITTING FROM A DIVOT MARK

The major goal in hitting a shot from a divot mark is to strike the ball without first contacting the turf behind the ball and thus allowing dirt between the clubface and the ball spoil the shot.

To successfully negotiate this sort of lie, one must materially lean his weight forward onto the outside of his left foot before he starts his swing. By more or less keeping his weight in this position during the swing, his club will go back and return to the ball at a sharp angle.

This abrupt angle of descent will cause the sole of the club to miss the high spot behind the ball while still pinching the ball for a solid contact.

It is true that this pinching action may cause the ball to strike the forward edge of the divot mark as it begins its flight, with the result that it will acquire so much top-spin that it will duck back to earth. Thus, it is important to take plenty of loft when hitting a shot from this sort of lie.

Solving Problems In The Sand

by Byron Nelson

Even if he never hits a single shot into a sand trap, the golfer who has trouble with bunker shots practically assures himself a higher-than-necessary score. Such a golfer seldom reaches his scoring potential because he must consciously avoid the sand. He must play ultra-safe golf, which is never conducive to low scoring.

Anyone can excel on shots from the sand, providing he or she is willing to devote some practice time toward mastering the proper technique.

In this article I will outline proper technique, but you must practice before it will pay dividends. You must practice enough to get the feel of how fast the ball will fly out of various types of sands. Only then will you be able to judge correctly the distance that various shots will fly from the sand.

You will discover after a short time that sand shots are really nothing to fear. You will approach these shots with confidence, and this is very important on all golf shots — especially those from sand.

Basically, there are only two major things that go wrong on sand shots. You either hit the ball too far or not far enough. Bad direction is seldom a factor.

If your problem is hitting sand shots past the hole, short of the pin, or both, I'd suggest you review the basic check-points for good sand shot play pinpointed in the following paragraphs.

1. Look at the spot where you want your club to enter the sand.

Many golfers unconsciously make the error of focusing on the ball before and during their swing as they would on a shot from the fairway. Since the club should enter *behind* the ball on sand explosion shots, it is obvious that fixing attention on the ball often will produce a "thin" shot that carries well past the pin, or even beyond the green.

Normally, the club should enter the sand about 1½"-2" behind the ball. This distance should vary with the length of the shot. On long sand shots you want the club to enter the sand closer to the ball than on short shots. The nearer to the ball the club enters, the farther the ball will fly.

Thus, distance on sand shots can be determined by the point of entry of the clubhead. I prefer this method of controlling distance to one governed by the length and force of the swing. I feel it is easier if I keep my swing fairly consistent on all sand shots and merely alter the point of entry.

2. Make sure you have a firm footing in the sand.

A lot of people just walk into the sand very daintily so that they don't make deep tracks. Please don't do that. Squirm your feet snugly into the sand so that they won't slip during your swing. It is against the rules to "test" the sand, but you can learn a lot about its texture and depth merely by taking a firm foothold.

3. Stand with your feet farther apart than normal for a shot of comparable length.

You need a wide base on sand shots to help insure against slipping and loss of balance.

4. Employ an open stance on all sand shots.

Such a stance finds the left foot (for right-handed players) pulled back farther than the right from the imaginary line to the target (Figure A). The ball should be played just back of the left heel but well forward of stance-center (Figure B).

This open stance will help you turn your body out of the way before the clubhead moves through the hitting area.

The open stance also encourages the club to move into the hitting area on an outside-in path. This, in effect, minimizes chances that the club will cut too deeply into the sand.

5. Address the ball on all normal sand shots with the clubface turned slightly open, facing a bit to the right of target.

The open clubface serves several useful purposes. It encourages the club to cut a shallow path in the sand. Thus, the clubhead enters well behind the ball but still moves readily through the sand. The open face also adds loft to the club. This loft comes in handy on many bunker shots. Finally, the open clubface helps counteract any tendency to pull the shot to the left that may result from the open stance and the outside-in club-head path (Figure C).

However, on shots wherein the ball is played from a "plugged" or buried lie, it probably will be necessary to address the ball with a square-to-target clubface. Then the club will cut deep enough into the sand to penetrate beneath the low-lying ball.

But always use an open stance on all sand shots.

A

B

C

6. Address the ball with more flex in your knees than on a normal fairway shot.

Additional flex in the knees is necessary on sand shots to insure freedom of movement during a swing that might otherwise be restricted by the lack of a firm foothold (Figure A). In fact, you should have more flex in your knees on sand shots than for any other type of golf stroke.

7. The sand shot swing should be short and definite with the hands and wrists quite firm.

I have found that the great sand trap players I've seen all grip short on the club and they do NOT use a lot of wrist (Figure B). They hold the club very firmly; take it back only a short distance and hit definitely through the sand.

If your sand shots are remaining in the bunker, it might well be that you are taking too long a swing and using too much wrist-action.

Your wrists should break a little — but very little — on the backswing. On the downswing your left arm and side should bring the club, cutting from the outside, across and beneath the ball. Imagine that your clubhead is a knife and that you are quickly slicing a thin piece off the side of an apple (Figure C). Don't cut into the core — unless your ball is buried. Make sure the knife continues through the apple in one swipe.

8. Stay down to the ball.

If your sand shots are flying farther than intended, the chances are excellent that you are not "staying down" to the ball and, as a result, your clubhead is not cutting under enough sand. I suggest that anyone with this problem check the following points:

— Make certain that your weight rests on your heels. If your weight is moving forward on your feet, you will have a tendency to raise your head.

— Keep your knees flexed. You should feel that you are squatting on sand shots.

— Employ a nice shoulder turn with some coiling of the hips. Too often players swing solely with their arms on sand shots. This also encourages lifting of the head, and the resulting lack of clubhead penetration into the sand.

— Keep your swing short. A long backswing may encourage a lifting of your head.

— Let the club's built-in loft raise the ball. The player who tries to scoop the shot into flight often lifts his body and thus fails to swing the clubhead into the sand.

9. Use a sand wedge.

This club features a wide sole that will cut through the sand readily without slicing too deeply. This club is made especially for sand shots and it will save you grief practically every time you take it out of the bag.

Solving Problems
On The Green

by Jack Burke, Jr.

There is probably nothing more exasperating in golf than a three-putt green. Unless you can put it out of your mind immediately, it can also affect the balance of your game. If you consistently three-putt, you may eventually find yourself quaking over the ball like a bowl of jello.

It is my opinion that golfers who consistently three-putt have no sense of touch. In that respect you can say that some people are born with putting talent and others are not, but this "feel" *can* be learned. Generally speaking, women seem to have a better sense of touch than most men among average golfers, possibly because they work more with their hands. Willie Sutton, the infamous safe-cracker, would probably have been a magnificent putter. He had a highly developed sense of touch.

Golfers who as kids pitched pennies to a line or flipped cards into a hat usually have developed a sense that helps them on the putting green. The same would hold true of pool or billiard players. Doug Ford even today plays a lot of pool when he finds his touch is slipping a bit, just to keep his "feel" sharp. Perhaps the fact that Bill Casper does a lot of precision line-casting as he fishes has something to do with his excellent putting record.

Judging distance and hitting the ball at the proper speed is over 90% of putting. Few will shank, top or toe a putt. It is possible on occasion to mis-hit for direction by pushing or pulling, but I am assuming that your mechanics of stroke-making are sound. If they are not, better get out and find a workable putting stroke.

Following are basic putting errors and the means of eliminating them.

THE PROBLEM OF "NO FEEL"

Not getting the long putts close enough to the hole in either distance or direction is due to lack of imagination. In other words, the golfer is trying to hit the ball into the hole but really has no "feel" for it.

Imagine that the hole is the size of a wash tub three feet in diameter. This may take some practice with your imagination but it can be developed. If the hole were actually this big there would be no question in your mind that you could hit it every time. By working on this you should be able, therefore, to place the ball within a foot-and-a-half of the hole almost every time — even from as far away as 60 feet.

THE PROBLEM OF POOR DISTANCE

Leaving the ball far short or hitting it well past the hole is a result of being unable to judge distance properly or not being able to imagine the right speed with which to hit the ball.

Imagine that you are rolling the ball to the hole with your hand. In fact, you might even practice doing this. If you find that you cannot get it close to the hole in this manner, you undoubtedly have an underdeveloped sense of touch. The same amount of force is used to stroke the ball with the putter as is used to roll the ball with the right hand. On longer putts I always walk at least half way to the hole and decide just about how fast I would roll the ball from that distance. Then I am able to hit the ball just about twice as hard and get it close to the hole.

THE PROBLEM OF NO CONFIDENCE

Lack of decisiveness in reading the break or roll of the green indicates a lack of confidence. Naturally you must start the ball out in the correct direction so that the break in the green will make the ball wind up near or in the hole.

Look the contour of the green over carefully and eliminate all alternative routes but one. By crouching down low behind the ball you should be able to tell which way the contour of the green slants. The ball must break right, left or go straight (which isn't often). Decide which way it breaks and by how much, and then stick to your decision. If you are not sure look it over until you *know* what the break is. One more tip. If the green is on a hill, be sure to check the surrounding terrain in case the whole green is on an angle. Seaside greens normally have added slope in the direction of the water.

THE STYLE PROBLEM

Lack of a good putting stroke, or lack of confidence in the stroke you are using, is fatal. Take a look at Arnold Palmer. The reason he is such a super putter at this time is that he knows he is going to stroke the ball with the same action every time he hits it. This breeds confidence. His left wrist breaks the same way every time — and *naturally*. He is comfortable, he is steady and he strokes the ball smoothly.

Find out the most natural and most comfortable way for *you* to putt, and then stick with it until you are sure you can hit the ball the same way every time. There are many grips, many stances and many strokes. One of them will be the most natural for you. Find it. It should allow you to feel comfortable. It should keep you steady so that there is no movement of the head or body. It should enable you to accelerate into the ball with the blade square to the target line every time. Putting styles vary with the individual. Note the different address positions used by Burke (upper left) Arnold Palmer (upper right) and Jack Nicklaus (below).

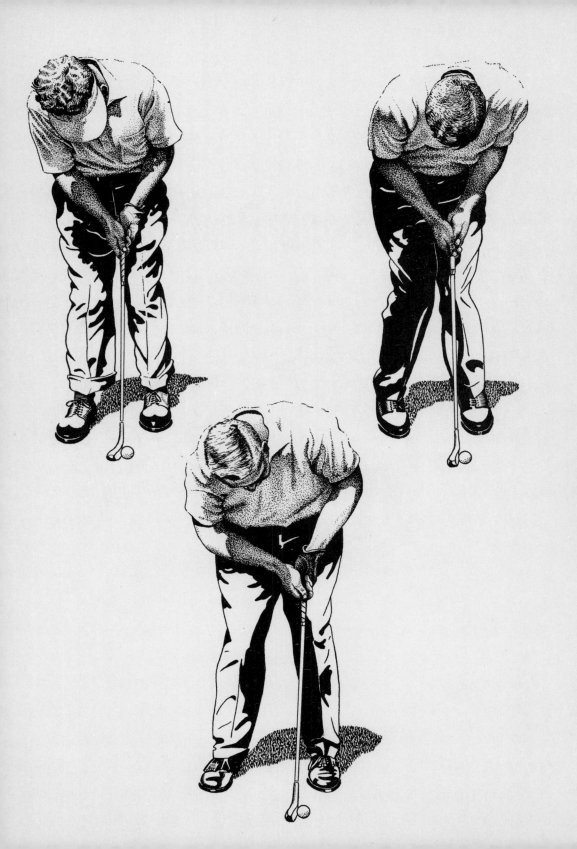

Solving Problems
In The Mind

by Jack Burke, Jr.

Extreme tension in golf — whether it be called choking, yipping or taking the gas — affects good players as often as it hits those of less skill. However, choking will have less detrimental effect on the better player who has a grooved swing that will withstand pressure.

Nerves hit the hardest when you are uncertain of your swing. When your swing pattern is not in the groove, you become apprehensive and start pressing. This throws the swing even more out of kilter. Under tension, a golfer with a normally fast swing starts swinging even faster, often to the point that he fails to complete his backswing.

When this happens to the expert golfer, he can quickly return his swing to normal merely by making a minor adjustment in, say, his grip or stance. Walter Hagen wasn't much for practicing, but he had the ability to correct his swing during a round. I think this was the big reason that he played with such confidence and freedom from tension.

When the less-skilled golfer becomes apprehensive about his swing, I advise that he try hitting his next few shots with less force. This will decrease the tempo of his swing and probably snap it back into the groove. At least it will offset the normal tendency to swing faster under pressure.

Apprehension about one's swing becomes magnified when the player competes in a tournament. Most average golfers make one big mistake in competition. They don't play the course; they play the event. They get all wrapped up in thoughts of winning trophies and getting their names in the paper and thus create additional pressure for themselves.

The best thing is to minimize the importance of the tournament. Don't try to be too good. Don't worry about winning or losing. Just figure you are out there to do a job. That is the attitude taken by the better competitors, and invariably it's the best competitor who wins the club championship — not necessarily the best shotmaker.

Some pros on the tour allow the money prize to become too important. That's why I feel that circuit newcomers who start with sufficient financial backing are in an ideal position to play their best. Ben Hogan was a great one for playing the course and the shot while more or less disregarding the importance of the event. The success of this philosophy is evident when one considers that he won the biggest pressure tournament of them all, the U.S. Open, four times.

There are certain times during a round when the player is exceptionally susceptible to pressure. One such time occurs when he is faced with a shot down a narrow fairway with trouble on both sides. Such a shot produces anxiety and often a bad swing.

I have found it helpful on such shots to imagine that the fairway is guarded on each side by a 75-foot high aluminum wall. When I have convinced myself that the "walls" will protect any stray shot I might hit, I am able to swing freely and usually produce a straight shot.

Tension also causes a hurried swing on shots to a small or narrow green, or one that is heavily guarded by hazards. I suggest that when this happens the golfer may be aiming at too small a target. It is ridiculous to expect pinpoint accuracy to a hole 4¼ inches in diameter from say, 150 yards away. It would take a rifle.

It is better to broaden the target. Imagine that the cup is almost as big as the entire green. This should reduce anxiety and allow a freer swing. In golf it sometimes helps to be a little nutty.

PUTTING AIDS

Tension in golf occurs most frequently on the greens, especially in the case of better-than-average players. Such anxiety in putting stems from the same source as on other shots — namely uncertainty or lack of confidence in your stroke; indecision as to how hard to hit the ball, and fear of missing the target.

Good putters don't think about results, good or bad. They just concern themselves with hitting the ball squarely.

On long putts tension often occurs because the player is aiming at such a small target. If you can imagine that the hole is, say three feet in diameter and then shoot for this "larger" target, chances are excellent that your nervousness will diminish and you will have fewer three-putt greens.

On short putts I find it eases tension to imagine that the path from the ball to the hole is discolored, say black or white, and about 4¼ inches (the width of the cup) wide. Then I just putt down the path.

Many players visualize a thread or narrow line running from the ball to the hole. Naturally it is easy to be concerned about your ability to putt down such a narrow line. It's much better to give yourself a wider path and thus increase your confidence that the ball will stay on line.

The better playing professionals all have certain ways to ease tension. Some pick up grass and test the wind. Others walk ahead of their ball to reassure themselves of the correct distance.

Jimmy Demaret swings his arms up and down. This keeps him loose; dries the perspiration on his hands and arms, and somehow encourages him to take a lighter grip on the club.

Some players, such as Dutch Harrison and Doug Sanders, relieve their tension by joking with the gallery or their caddies. On the other hand, Ben Hogan doesn't talk to anyone when he is competing. Hogan becomes tense when his concentration is broken. He feels a sort of loss of contact with the game when this happens.

I guess I'm sort of like Hogan in this respect. I'm less tense and at my best when I'm completely devoting my attention to shot-planning. Conversation takes my mind off the next shot and then I feel uneasy.

Thus, positive thoughts about what I plan to do on my next shot are, for me, the best therapy against choking. I have little time to get nervous when my mind is occupied with the job at hand. Maybe this protection against choking will also work for you.

Solving Problems
On The Scorecard

by Paul Runyan

Whether your problem be bogies or double bogies — or both — the situation can be relieved by a common-sense review of your golfing habits. The purpose of this article is to help you make such an analysis.

There are certain times during a round of golf when players are especially susceptible to bad holes. These include (1) early in the round, (2) after a break between nines, (3) near the end of a round and (4) after a string of good holes or (5) after an especially bad hole or bad break.

EARLY IN THE ROUND

In golf more than in any other sport, players are likely to start without proper warm-up. This often results in several bogies before the player has a proper feel of his game.

Mr. Adrian McManus, a friend of long standing and the godfather of my youngest son, Jeff, is a wonderful example of how to properly prepare for a round of golf.

It has always been his custom to arrive at the club at least an hour before his game for a leisurely warm-up of about 30 to 45 minutes. As a result he spoils fewer rounds with an early string of bogies than any other amateur golfer I can name. Of course, today's fine professionals are sticklers for a proper warm-up.

I feel that the order in which a warm-up is carried out is important. Chipping and putting have a tendency to constrict the muscles of the back, shoulders, neck and arms and, therefore, should be practiced before one hits his or her short, medium, and long irons and woods in that order. Drives should be the last shots practiced before going to the first tee.

THE NINE-HOLE BREAK

Frequently a break between nines will produce a string of bogies soon thereafter.

I can remember Jimmy Thomson, the "siege gun" of our time, often shooting a fine front nine, hastily gulping down two ice cold soft drinks and then wondering why he could not sustain his string of pars and birdies beyond the ninth hole.

It is vital to keep the muscles warm and supple for the entire round. Once muscles cool and stiffen during a pause for lunch or a visit to the 19th hole between nines, they are more difficult to re-warm than before the round initially began.

So avoid those bogies early on the second nine by leisurely completing your round without a between-nine interruption.

LATE IN THE ROUND

Often late-round bogies stem from a player's being tired, both mentally and physically. Golfers should anticipate this condition and get proper rest the night before and eat a good breakfast or lunch prior to the game.

I also think that golfers should carry a plastic vial of honey in their bags, and take a few sips from it on the last nine. Honey can work miracles in warding off fatigue and the jangled nerves that go with being tired.

Of course, one of the finest ways to avoid bogies at any time is to keep in top physical condition. I feel that this is the principal reason why Gene Littler can come back so quickly from occasional slumps. Keeping in good shape seems to be a way of life for Gene. Thus he suffers no nerve irritation due to training as incurred by some golfing athletes.

AFTER GOOD HOLES

It has been said militarily that a strong offense is a powerful defense. I feel this maxim applies most assuredly in golf. How often I have seen a fine player amass a string of pars and birdies and then blow his chances for a record score by starting to play safe.

Developing a negative attitude is the surest way to produce bad holes. The very best way to protect a lead or a good partial score is to play each hole as a separate entity and to attack it as if you were behind and trying to make up ground.

In short, think about making some birdies — or pars if you are a higher handicap player — and the bogies will most likely disappear.

AFTER A BAD HOLE

Too often an extremely bad hole or a bad break will produce a string of bogies.

Ideally, after a bad hole the player should forget his past mistakes. This is good advice, but often difficult to carry out unless the player can focus his attention on something other than the past errors.

To erase unpleasant memories the player should immediately adopt a positive attitude by planning his strategy on the next hole.

His first action upon reaching the next tee should be to note the pin position on the green. Then he should decide where his tee shot should finish to provide the best opening to the green.

Such positive thinking should continue on the second shot. The player should decide where on the green his ball should finish to leave him an easy putt.

Such planning should be a habit on all holes, but it is especially important after a bad one when the golfer needs a crutch to banish negative thoughts.

I recently played a nine-hole exhibition match and gave a teaching clinic in Grass Valley, Calif., a delightful small town in the timber and mining country of the Sierra Nevada foothills.

Before playing each stroke during the round, I lectured to the gallery as to how I thought the shot should be planned and executed. My execution was of questionable skill — I missed four of the nine greens on my approach shot. However, I had planned the shots so that if they should miss the green I would still be in position to recover easily. As a result I had no bogies and one birdie for a very respectable score.

When it comes to avoiding bogies through careful planning, Ben Hogan gets my nod as the king of them all. Of course he had the shots to back up his planning; but if anything contributed to Hogan's right to be called golf's all-time greatest player — which I think he deserves — it was his highly developed ability to pre-plan each round, every hole and all shots.

ANALYZING YOUR GAME

It may be that a golfer's bogies do not follow a pattern of occurring at specific periods during a round. If this is the case, if bad holes creep in without apparent rhyme or reason, the player should take counsel with himself — and preferably some good instructor — to discover the causes of the inconsistencies.

When such a search is made, it may be discovered that the bogies occur when the player misses more greens than normal.

In such cases it may be that the golfer's tee shots are so wild that he leaves himself little or no chance to reach the green in regulation figures. If this is the case, obviously some driving instruction would be warranted.

If bad driving is not the culprit, the player should determine to what extent his approach shots miss the greens. If they are far off-line, it would seem that practice and instruction on the irons would be required. If the player's approach shots just barely miss the greens, and he still takes three or more shots to hole out, it would seem time to work on the chipping and pitching or short putting.

Now let's take the case of the player who hits a goodly number of the greens but still has more bogies than is reasonable. This player needs to acquire some additional skill in the art of approach putting because it is evident that he is taking too many three-putt greens.

For the player who is weak on sand shots a ball in a trap will most likely result in a bogey unless this player works on this phase of his game.

I feel that a player who understands the sand shot, has a good sand club and is willing to devote a few minutes each day to practice from the sand to acquire a feeling for distance should, in a short time, be able to lay the ball up for one putt three times out of four from a normal lie.

SHORT PUTT TROUBLE?

If a player finds that his recovery shots are suitable, but that bogies still occur in an over-abundance, he obviously should work on his short putts.

Let's consider the player who does not play certain types of shots well. One such example is my good friend Chandler Harper, who was — and probably still is — one of golf's finest "cut" shot players. He could make a shot bend to the right without any difficulty.

However, Chandler did not have a flair for making shots "draw" to the left. When he encountered a course with several holes that doglegged to the left or one on which many pins were placed on the left side of the greens, Chandler would likely come up with too high a percentage of bogies to obtain a satisfactory score.

The opposite could be said of Zell Eaton, who possessed one of golf's most consistent draw games, but who encountered bogie trouble when he faced doglegs to the right and pin placements on that side of greens.

These examples underline the fact that golf is certainly a highly specialized game — so specialized that even the greatest players fall prey to bogies. However, I do feel that any golfer who is willing to work and take instruction can ease his bogey problems by a careful analysis of his game as I have outlined.